What Was I Thinking?

What Was I Thinking?

THE SUBCONSCIOUS IN DECISION-MAKING

C. Gates

Library of Congress Control Number: 2014907194
ISBN: Hardcover   978-1-4990-0410-6
                Softcover   978-1-4990-0406-9
                eBook   978-1-4990-0411-3

This book was printed in the United States of America.

Rev. date: 05/23/2014

To order additional copies of this book, contact:
Xlibris LLC
1-888-795-4274
www.Xlibris.com
Orders@Xlibris.com
616223

Contents

Acknowledgments

Dedicated to Javi who impresses and challenges me with his clear thinking. Your Mother and I surely are lucky to have you in our lives.

Also, thanks to amazing Bob, my best man and continual inspiration, Bird for keeping me grounded, Tom and Lee for enduring my constant references to the book and their helpful thoughts on what to put into it, Danielle for the access to the research materials that helped focus my efforts, Jessie and her family for giving me so many happy memories to go to, Pat and Sabrina for their early interest, Ron for his statistical advice, J. double ya (W) for his support in turning things around, Chris and daughter for their educated comments, Nelida and Elizabeth for getting this started, though it has been a different animal than the one they requested, Matt and all the Whitpain folks that that have brought me Thursday night joy, and Lisa who taught me that if you can't write it, you don't understand it.

Out of my head

Into yours

Introduction

Reason is the slave of the passions. David Hume.

The heart has arguments with which the logic of
the mind is not acquainted. Blaise Pascal.

This is a book about how your fast, intuitive, subconscious mind influences the decisions you make every day. Unlike its slow, rational, conscious partner, we carry on pretty much unaware of its existence. Increasing that awareness has been the goal of a number of rather clever experiments that have allowed us a glimpse into the operation of the subconscious. Its affect on your judgment and decisions just may surprise you.

The subconscious mind has some very peculiar properties. It works relatively well compared to our rational mind when there is little information, and perhaps even better when there is too much. It has reflex-like quickness, unfettered by having to take the time to be reflective[1].

---

[1]   Yogi Berra, When your come to a fork in the road, take it.

Kahneman[2] calls this characteristic of the subconscious WYSIATI, What You See Is All There Is. It informs your rational brain what it senses. It doesn't judge but does try to make sense out of dangerous or surprising conditions to send a cohesive message to your conscious mind. It then moves on to the next moment where it continues working to keep your conscious mind informed of its updated surroundings.

The subconscious mind employs a variety of quick and dirty guides, referred to as heuristics, to support fast decision making. Heuristics are subconscious guides that answer the general question, "If this, then what?" The Availability Heuristic, for example, instructs us on how to estimate the relative probability of an event. By this guide, if the event comes to mind more easily than another, it probably occurs more frequently. While this rule of thumb[3] makes sense and is generally useful, it can also lead to bad decisions from the influence of other factors that can affect

---

[2]   Daniel Kahneman is the psychologist who, together with deceased Amos Tversky, won the 2002 Nobel Prize in Economic Sciences. In his eye opening 1994 book "Inevitable Illusions : How Mistakes of Reason Rule Our Minds" Piattelli-Palmarini wrote "I am persuaded that, sooner or later, Amos Tversky and Daniel Kahneman will win the Nobel Prize for economics." Good call.

[3]   (From the Barr Labs court decision on the inappropriate use of re-testing in pharmaceutical laboratories http:// www.leagle.com/decision/19931270812FSupp458_11169, footnote 3, "The Court chooses not to rely on the phrase "rule of thumb." Although apparently a common and useful phrase, as evidenced by the frequency with which it appears in the hearing transcript, this expression is derived from the historical common law right of the husband to beat his wife with a switch, provided it was "no thicker than his thumb." "Caitlin E. Borgman, Note, Battered Women's Substantive Due Process Claims: Can Orders of Protection Defeat DeShaney?, 65 N.Y.U.L.Rev. 1280, 1281 n. 3.

our estimate of frequency, such as how interesting the event is.

If your subconscious mind's (System 1, or simply S1) operation finds something that clashes with its expectations, it could signal an alarm for your conscious mind (System 2, S2) to focus on these signals. If the situation is urgent enough, S1 may react immediately (flight, frozen fright, or fight) and not wait to be approved by S2. While we would like to think that an S2 reaction will be unbiased, logical, and reasonable, there will be times when it is none of the above. When we sense a gut feeling, a hunch, uneasiness, or an opportunity, we are motivated to resolve it. Heuristics that are so valuable most of the time by supporting quick decisions are also often the culprits of questionable behavior such as neglect of critical data. Putting the pedal to the metal supports the need for speed, but at what cost? As we shall see, heuristics tend to bias the evaluation of risk in predictable directions.

The S1's mode of operation works on the level of individual anecdotes; stories, not averages or other generalities, are its food for thought. It works with concrete concepts, not abstract.[4] Our intuitive mind doesn't see averages or imagine what is not there. Let's look at a couple of simple examples of the S1 at work.

1. How you present a question (referred to as framing), should not affect the answer. Consider the question of what speed a car was going when it made contact with another car. After participants in an experiment viewed a film of the accident, they gave a higher estimate of velocity when the question was posed as "How fast was the car travelling when

---

[4]   Taleb Black pg 132 "Most of all we favor the narrated. Alas, we are not manufactured, in our current edition of the human race, to understand abstract matters—we need context."

it smashed into the other car?" compared to "How fast was the car travelling when it hit the other car?" As well, those exposed to the word "smashed" were more likely to have the associated false memory of broken glass.

2. An estimate of frequency, which participants could observe directly, should not be influenced by information that is irrelevant to the estimate. A child was filmed answering questions. Some of her answers were wrong. Prior to this, participants in the experiment were shown pictures of her either in a poor part of town, or in a more advantaged area. When asked how many mistakes the girl made, estimates were higher for the group that had seen her in the poor area.[5]

3. It should not matter that you were asked to write down the last four digits of your SS# prior to estimating how many street names in New York City begin with the letter "T", but it does. Those with Higher SS#s give higher number of 'T street' estimates. More on this under the subject of Anchoring.

These short and simple examples illustrate the occasionally strange and biased decisions we make in certain situations. While it has been difficult to avoid making these common errors, the first step in trying to do so is to know that they exist and why. Trying to better understand why we form biased beliefs and make poor choices will be the goal of much of what follows.

Intuition and gut feelings have been evolutionarily selected for because they often have made the difference between the quick and the dead. Nevertheless, the influence of these same mechanisms on our judgment/

---

[5]   Myers pg 40

decision making process can sometimes be inappropriate in a world now far removed from that of our distant ancestors where these feelings tracked and were a normal reaction to experience. Their daily challenges and needs were different and more immediate than those we now experience. Ongoing experiments are beginning to unravel the effects of these phenomena and reveal their purpose.

Heuristics provide a set of tools for making quick judgments and decisions. It can also be understood from our internal storytelling that these tools are designed to achieve what Kahneman called "cognitive ease". We'll soon see how that's done.

This book grew out of an interest in risk analysis in the pharmaceutical industry. While researching this subject, a reference for the psychology of judgment and decision making authored by Scott Plous caught my eye and my interest. Reading his book started me on a journey to better understand why certain decisions we make appear, on first look, inexplicable. I believe what I've gathered together here will be of general interest and is intended to avail you of some thoughts and findings on the purposes of our rational and our intuitive minds. My hope is that you will enjoy the read, and I think you will if you are curious about how and why we decide to do what we do. My goal is that by the end of this book you will be better prepared to answer the sometimes awkward question, What *was* I thinking?

Decisions made while performing risk analysis in the pharmaceutical industry are expected to reflect good science. Unfortunately, the ubiquitous nature of the subconscious with its built in subjective biases makes it hard to control and so will sometimes color our best efforts at being objective. From time to time I will very briefly refer to some of the simpler graphical and statistical tools that the FDA expects the pharmaceutical industry to use to reduce subjectivity in risk analysis. We will see that we probably underestimate the role of the unconscious in using these 'objective' tools.

My informal definition of risk relates to the unpredictable outcomes of our choices. How we balance the aversion to risk with the probability of benefits varies between us and within us. What goes into making these choices? Much is derived from the unconscious. Some risks, like the possibility of regret for not bringing your umbrella on a rainy day or not buying insurance on a busted appliance are relatively small compared with decisions on, say, how to protect the earth from climate change. Be they big or small, we can use all the help we can get in making effective decisions. I would like to think the following will get us to reflect a little more about how we think and how we act on those judgments that affect us and others.

As a bit of housekeeping, I will use the terms unconscious and subconscious as equivalents. Unconscious seems to be the choice of professionals in this field, though the meaning seems to have changed from that popularized by Freud some time ago. The unconscious mind is analogous to Pascal's *heart* which we will refer to as Kahneman's 'System 1' or just S1. Pascal's *mind* is essentially Kahneman's[6] 'System 2'(S2), the rational mind. I have included a Glossary that I hope will clarify some the terms used in this book. Words within [ ] are my comments when used within another's quote.

A word on quotations. I have collected quotes over the last several years, trying to focus on those that are short and hopefully insightful and witty. Many of these seemed to nicely fit the objectives of this book. Many others may leave you wondering, 'what was he thinking?' I have not tried to assure the correct credit for these epigrams. I would like to think that a thought should be able to stand on its own, regardless of its author.

---

6   Kahneman 2011 pg 20. Adopted from Stanovich and West.

Chapter 1

THE DECISION

Whither the weather?

Mistakes live in the neighborhood of
truth and therefore delude us.
Rabi Tagore[7]

A life and death decision

On January 28, 1986, the Space Shuttle *Challenger* broke
apart 73 seconds into its flight, leading to the deaths of its

---

[7] We have not learned to live with our mistakes, so we find a way
to hide them from our own sight. We fool ourselves to better
fool others. This works best when it is not obvious, that is,
when it is not overdone, not far from the truth, reasonable but
wrong. We are most easily made April Fools when the practical
joke seems most plausible.

seven crew members. The investigation for the cause of that explosion exposed a decision making environment where safety competed with cost and other concerns.[8] As part of the risk analysis investigations for this disaster that linked O-ring performance under cold conditions with the flight failure, Nobel Laureate (Physics 1965) Richard Feynman wrote:

> "It appears that there are enormous differences of opinion as to the probability of a failure with loss of vehicle and of human life. The estimates range from roughly 1 in 100 to 1 in 100,000. The higher figures come from the working engineers, and the very low figures from management. What are the causes and consequences of this lack of agreement? Since 1 part in 100,000 would imply that one could put a Shuttle up each day for 300 years expecting to lose only one, we could properly ask 'What is the cause of management's fantastic faith in the machinery?'[9]

---

[8]   Tufte, Visual Explanations, pg 52 "For the Challenger, there were substantial pressures to get it off the ground as quickly a possible: an unrealistic and over-optimistic flight schedule based on the premise that launches were a matter of routine . . . the difficulty for the rocket-maker (Morton Thiokol) to deny the demands of its major client (NASA); and a preoccupation with public relations and media event (there was a possibility of a televised conversation between the orbiting astronaut-teacher Christa McAuliffe and President Regan during his State of the Union address that night, 10 hours after the launch.)"

[9]   Gigerenzer Rationality, pg 150. Perhaps what Gerd Gigerenzer learned on visit to the DASA (rocket) factory where Ariane rockets were made helps to explain the disparity. The tour guide answered his question of the risk of a launch failure as having a security factor of 99.6%. This seemed incongruous with the fact that of 94 flights, there had been eight accidents. The guide went on to explain that they did not use launch

We have also found that certification criteria used in Flight Readiness Reviews often develop a gradually decreasing strictness. The argument that the same risk was flown before without failure is often accepted as an argument for the safety of accepting it again. Because of this, obvious weaknesses are accepted again and again, sometimes without a sufficiently serious attempt to remedy them,[10] or to delay a flight because of their continued presence".[11]

What *was* NASA thinking? It's hard to know, but it appeared they had made up their minds to launch, and were looking to confirm that posture. Perhaps the pressures to blast off were just too much to consider the possibility of waiting for warmer weather. Delay was not an option. "A high-level NASA official responded that he was 'appalled' by the recommendation not to launch and indicated that the rocket maker, Morton Thiokol, should reconsider, even though this was Thiokol's only no-launch recommendation in 12 years."[12] It would take better arguments than those presented by the Morton Thiokol engineers to convince NASA otherwise. Why? As we will see in chapter 4, once

---

failures in their calculations. They based the 99.6 figure on the reliability of the construction of the individual parts.

When we speak of probability, we need to know if we are referring to subjective confidence, or are if we are talking about probability derived from design, such as the construction of a gambling die.

[10] Trivers pg 204 "As Feynman noted, this is like playing Russian roulette and feeling safer after each pull of the trigger fails to kill you."

[11] http://www.ralentz.com/old/space/feynman-report.html

[12] Tufte pg 39. Also, this can-do attitude reflects a certain familiarity with launching. Been there, done that. A little cool weather was insufficient to justify a delay in the launch.

we have convinced ourselves that something is true (for example, no danger ahead) we will defend that view, often with a bias to accumulate confirmatory evidence in favor of a predetermined judgment, rather than taking the more scientifically sound approach of obtaining information that challenges the hypothesis.

A second factor that may have biased their decision to launch was the disregard of data from previous flights for higher temperature O-ring performance that would have added context and possibly changed their analysis. Data on O ring performance at varying temperatures was available but poorly presented. The proper presentation of the silent evidence, the warm weather, low failure rate data (not done in this particular case) would have provided a contrasting back drop to the few worst (low temperature) cases.[13] Without it, the arguments were weak.[14] The warm weather

---

[13]   Tuft pg 43 "Left out were the other 22 previous shuttle flights and their temperature variation and O-ring performance. A careful look at such evidence would have made the dangers of a cold launch clear."

[14]   Trivers page 202 "To prevent themselves—or others—from seeing this, the safety unit performed the following mental operation. They said that sixteen flights showed no damage and were thus irrelevant and could be excluded from further analysis. This is extraordinary in itself—one never wishes to throw away data, especially when it is so hard to come by. Since some damage occurred during high-temperature takeoffs, (NASA argued) temperature at takeoff could be ruled out as a cause." The correct argument or hypothesis to test was not whether damage to O-rings can occur at higher temperatures, it was whether damage is more likely at lower temperatures. NASA's argument was too simplified. They turned the variable severity data into attribute data, which loses information. They were looking for ways to confirm their predetermined decision, not necessarily using the data to challenge it. They 'selected' the data that supported no relation between launch temperature and O-ring failure. Remove the higher launch temperature damage data so that there is nothing to compare

data with a near total absence of O-ring problems was insufficiently presented. Who needs to see data analyzed for events at high temperatures when we are trying to prepare for a low temperature launch? The correct approach to analyzing problems should assure us that not only do we obtain information about what's happening when a problem occurs, but also when it doesn't. An example of the need to have both for (O-ring event) and against (no O-ring event) the inclusion of certain data is addressed in Appendix 1.

The O-ring failure data was thin, and this high temperature data omission made it thinner. As Tufte wrote[15]: "The flights without damage provide the statistical leverage necessary to understand the effects of temperature. Numbers become evidence by being in relation to." The significance of near complete lack of failures in warm weather, what the 'in relation to' was, was lost to the argument. See Appendix 6 for how non-events are incorporated into calculations of probability.

This omission of data was no oversight. The Morton Thiokol engineers tried in vain to convince NASA that this was an accident waiting to happen. However, this relationship between temperature and O-ring performance was *not* clearly presented in the 13 charts and tables prepared by Morton Thiokol engineers and used the night

---

with the lower temperature damage, and this argument is lost." This example is now taught in elementary statistics texts as an example of how not to do statistics. It is also taught in courses on optimal (or suboptimal) data presentation since, even while arguing against a flight, the engineers at Thiokol, the company that built the O-ring, presented their evidence in such a way as to invite rebuttal." They didn't plot the data, they just put it in tables or lists. The classic advice for someone who has to analyze data: graph it, graph it, graph it.

[15]   Tufte pg 44

prior to the launch to support the case that the temperature would be too low to launch.

"The charts were unconvincing; the arguments against the launch failed; the Challenger blew up."[16]

Decision making based on ignorance

Instead of the objective scientific discussion you would expect in such a situation, NASA was leaning to launch, in direct opposition to the sub-contractor engineers' concern with safety. These two camps of thought, with NASA owning the right to make the final decision, shifted the burden of proof from NASA assuming danger and having the engineers prove safety, to NASA assuming safety and having the engineers prove danger. From this it followed that if there were insufficient evidence to prove danger, safety would be assumed. The engineers were effectively on trial, assumed guilty of being wrong until they could prove their case of danger lurking, to their judge and jury, NASA. NASA's arguing to launch on the basis of ignorance[17]

---

16   Tufte pg 40

17   The appeal to ignorance is a logical fallacy of irrelevance, occurring when one claims that something is true only because it hasn't been proved false, or that something is false only because it has not been proved true. A claim's truth or falsity depends on supporting or refuting evidence to the claim, not the lack of support for a *contrary* or *contradictory* claim. (*Contrary* claims can't both be true but both can be false, unlike *contradictory* claims. "Jones was in Chicago at the time of the robbery" and "Jones was in Miami at the time of the robbery" are *contrary* claims–assuming there is no equivocation with 'Jones' or 'robbery'. "Jones was in Chicago at the time of the robbery" and "Jones was not in Chicago at the time of the robbery" are contradictory. A claim *is* proved true if its contradictory is proved false, and vice-versa.)

(insufficient results from launches at low temperature) runs contrary to sound scientific thinking.[18]

This kind of thinking parallels[19] what frequently occurs in hypothesis testing. If the results of a test indicate that the difference between two groups of data is insignificant, it is often thought that you can use this to conclude they are the same or equivalent. Not true. In such a case, all you can truly say is that there was insufficient information to declare there was a difference.

Conversely, just because two numbers are not the same, does not mean that they are different.

The Challenger story gives this book its first real world example of scientists not behaving scientifically. If asked, NASA would have probably denied that the political environment affected their decision. Also, they most likely would have denied they were looking for evidence that confirmed (by not looking at the higher temperature flights that had a minimum of O-ring failures) their decision. Their decisions were more influenced by their unconscious System 1 than they were aware of.

Challenging your belief

As another example of belief based on the lack of evidence, consider the once widely accepted hypothesis that all swans are white. The truth had to await the observation

---

[18] A short example of this kind of invalid thinking based on insufficient evidence:
No one has been able to disprove the existence of God. (nothing follows from this)
Therefore: (there is no reason for the "therefore")
God exists.

[19] Decreasing the power of the test to indicate that the null hypothesis (of no temperature effect) is fundamentally wrong because it decreases the number of results considered.

of a black swan in Australia to test or 'prove' the hypothesis. As Albert Einstein put it, "No amount of experimentation [such as the observation of white swans] can ever prove me right [that non-white swans don't exist]; a single experiment [observation of a black swan] can prove me wrong." With this in mind, it is generally understood that the defense of a belief is served best by challenging the belief. Search for contradictions, inconsistencies, and exceptions that prove (test) the rule. If this approach can survive the skeptics, both its chances of being right and our confidence in its truth are consequently enhanced.

Lack of proof that your interpretation *is not* correct doesn't affect the probability that it *is* correct. Your truth is not necessarily The Truth. Absence of evidence is not necessarily evidence of absence. If the scientific approach to evaluating a hypothesis is to challenge it, not to pile on instances where it works, why wasn't that approach followed in the Challenger disaster? Why weren't the worst actual cases of low temperature damage used more convincingly to challenge the hypothesis that a cold launch would be safe? Why weren't the rocket scientists thinking scientifically?

By not taking into account the silent (warm weather result of past flights) evidence,[20] there was less support against the launch, and so it became more acceptable to launch. By this reasoning, if we can't disprove there's no bear in the bush (we can't see through the entire bush), then, by the erroneous argument from ignorance, we

---

[20]   Taleb Black pg 302. The evidence against the belief or hypothesis. "Fallacy of silent evidence: Looking at history we do not see the full story, only the rosier parts of the process." By rosier he was referring to the evidence in favor of the hypothesis or belief. This is the confirmation bias at work. When it comes to the memory process, we reconstuct memories to include support for what our current thinking is. We misremember to our advantage.

should act as if there is no bear in the bush.[21] How did that kind of thinking work out for you Darwin Award[22] winners?

Another reason for this misguided thinking is due to the problem of induction. The problem comes from predicting a general result based on past individual results without the knowledge of why past results are what they are. Knowledge of history without knowledge of cause and effect should be more cause for concern than it generally is. Tom Turkey spends every day of his life being fed and cared for. What could possibly go wrong? All evidence points to tomorrow being just another day like yesterday. Not knowing the context of what inevitably happened to other turkeys on Thanksgiving Day will lead to a false sense of security for poor old Tom.

As stated earlier by Feynman, as flights went well in spite of risks, those risks became progressively more familiar, and so less worrisome. We became habituated; it was no longer a matter of concern.

Bearing in mind that there have been conflicting versions of the Challenger pre-flight evaluation of risks, particularly the risks of O-ring failure, the following graph shows the history of O-ring failure as a function of temperature prior to the accident.[23]

---

[21] This is called the Argument from ignorance, also known as *argumentum ad ignorantiam* or "appeal to ignorance" (where "ignorance" stands for: "lack of evidence to the contrary"). In a test of the null hypothesis of no difference, if there is insufficient evidence to show a statistical difference, this does not prove there is no difference. Arguments from ignorance infer that a proposition (it's ok to launch) is true from the fact that it is not known (no evidence to the contrary) to be false.

[22] Darwin awards have been given to those individuals who did something (such as stupidly assuming safety in a risky situation) to remove their genes from further contribution to the gene pool.

[23] No such scattergrams were among the 13 charts used the night before launch to evaluate the effect of temperature on O-rings. Tuft pg 52

O-RING PERFORMANCE

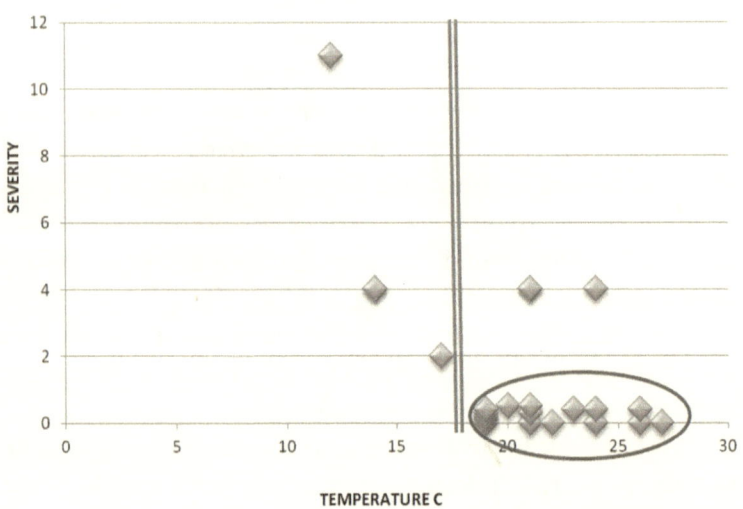

TEMPERATURE C

Does the graph suggest to you a possible relationship between temperature and severity of damage? The values *in the oval* are basically results of little or no damage.[24] Remove those from the graph and there seems to be a less certain relation between temperature and reliability.[25] With the encircled data included, the conclusion is clearer that higher temperatures (values to the right of the vertical bar) yield less severe damage to O-rings. The fatal decision to launch in weather much colder than any of the previous flights might have been influenced by which graphs were shown to the decision makers. If the assumption or actual request for data had been along the lines of 'show me at what temperature) the rings fail', a graph might just have been prepared for failures only, severity >1, and that would

---

[24] Remake, pg 45, of Tufte's scattergram.
[25] When just the failures are displayed, the high value at about 12 degrees looks like an anomaly, an outlier, an isolated event.

result in an inadequate context for evaluation, leading to the erroneous decision that it was justified to launch in the cold.

Kaleb refers to data such as that circled on the graph as 'silent evidence'. The NASA smoke screen proposition was that there was little evidence of O-ring failures in the cold. There was also little evidence of O-rings *not* failing at low temperatures. Again, the absence of evidence does not imply that there is evidence of absence. The absence of strong evidence of failure in the cold does not mean there is evidence of no failure. If there had been more, colder launches to obtain data from, and had there been the expected failures occurred among those, we would correctly claim there was evidence for increased risk of failure at low launch temperatures.

In the post explosion investigation, the integrity of the pre-launch charts prepared by the engineers came to be questioned. One had a CYA that read: "Information on this page was prepared to support an oral presentation and cannot be considered complete without the oral discussion."[26] As an example of NASA's mind set was the data 'treatment' for one of the 24 rockets that had been lost at sea. Though the O-ring damage for that rocket was unknown, it was listed as having no damage. To repeat Feynman's probing query, "What is the cause of management's fantastic faith in the machinery?" What Were They Thinking?

Tuft pg 40, on the fact that the charts provided pre launch by the Morton Thiokol engineers did not indicate an author with whom follow up could be done, wrote: "Readers can also recall what they know about the author's reputation and credibility. And so even a chart title, if it lacks appropriate documentation, might well provoke some suspicion about the evidence to come." Here we begin

---

[26] Tufte pg 47

to see how emotions and other unexpected, seemingly nonscientific, factors influence decision making. In this example, where truthful presentation of the data should have been taken for granted, a moment of doubt about an innocent omission may have casted a twisted halo effect (see glossary) on the remainder of the argument.[27]

It would seem that NASA officials were locked into their faulty initial feeling that it was ok to launch. What appeared to support this decision was the deficiency of disconfirming evidence. They reasoned that lack of information against their position, was effectively information in favor of their position. This is the same argument as the bear in the bush scenario. NASA was willing to make a type 2 error, that without more information, they would assume that the rustling bush was not something to be wary of. When lives are at stake, it's better to risk making the conservative type 1 error where you assume it's a bear (worst case) even if it's not. You take precautions and live to see another day. NASA decided there wasn't enough information to warrant their worry. They were dead wrong.

Rather than showing evidence to defend their decision, their logic seemed to be to show that since there was no strong evidence that cold would affect the O-rings, then they are not affected by the cold. Unfortunately, since flights had never occurred in the expected extreme launch conditions of near freezing temperature, the data didn't convincingly show beyond a reasonable doubt a relationship between temperature and O-ring performance.

Why was it so difficult to influence NASA officials to stop the launch? In general, why is it so difficult for any of us to change our minds? We will return to this question in chapter 4.

---

[27]   Tufte pg 40

Chapter 2

HEURISTICS, INTUITION, AND COGNITIVE EASE

Knowing what Thou knowest not is in a sense
Omniscience.

-Piet Hein, poet and scientist (1905-1996)

"Good science is more than the mechanics of research and experimentation. Good science requires that scientists look inward to contemplate the origin of their thoughts. The failures of science do not begin with flawed evidence or fumbled statistics; they begin with personal self-deception and an unjustified *sense of knowing*."

"It certainly takes bravery to remain skeptical; it takes inordinate courage to introspect, to confront oneself, to accept one's limitations—scientists are seeing more and more evidence that we are specifically designed by Mother Nature to fool ourselves."[28]

Fast is fine, but accuracy is everything.—Wyatt Earp

Emotions have taught mankind to reason. Marquis De Vauvenargues

"We know the nature and quality of our thoughts via feelings, not reason. Feelings such as certainty, conviction, rightness and wrongness, clarity, and faith arise out of involuntary mental sensory systems that are integral and inseparable components of the thoughts that they qualify".[29]

Overview

In this chapter we will spend time on some of the reasons, many unconscious, why our thinking, our beliefs, don't always work as rationally as we might expect. We will see how the success of our thinking can be estimated in part by how well it works at putting our minds at cognitive ease (CE), though this ease often comes with a sacrifice of data accuracy, completeness, and reliability.

Defining the rules of cognitive and behavioral algorithms: Heuristics as epigrams

"The technical definition of a heuristic is a simple procedure that helps find adequate, though often imperfect, answers to difficult questions. The word comes

---

[28]   Taleb Fooled preface pg x
[29]   Burton pg 139

from the same root as eureka ['I've found it']."[30] 'Eureka', as you may recall, is what Archimedes yelled while jumping out of his bath and running down the streets after solving a puzzle about how to test whether a golden crown really was solid gold.

"The word heuristic comes from philosophy by way of computer science. Computer scientists realized early on that some problems are too complex even for high-powered computers. These problems might have perfect solutions, but the computers would have to crunch away for weeks or months or years to figure them out. Consequently, computer scientists devised shortcut algorithms (a.k.a. heuristics) that produced 'good-enough' solutions in a more reasonable time. As with these computer programs, cognitive heuristics offer us a trade-off: we accept some imperfections in our decisions for the practicality of getting the job done."[31]

Baron credits the mathematician George Polya with the popularization of the term heuristics.[32] Polya wrote in his 1945 "How to Solve it": "[heuristics is] . . . reasoning not regarded as final and strict but as provisional and plausible only, whose purpose is to discover the solution of the present problem." I want to emphasize that these heuristics are suited to pleasing the mind, but can also be misleading by debilitating the accuracy of our estimates and predictions.

Heuristics are those rules of thumb that we are generally unaware of yet still serve to affect our decision making. These rules are useful especially at the extreme

---

[30]   K2011 pg 98
[31]   Herbert pg 12
[32]   Baron pg 53

highs[33] and lows[34] of information availability where data is
so lacking, or so overwhelming that subjective intuitions are
welcomed advisors and play a significant role. They work
efficiently, below the radar, giving us a 'gut feeling' of the
best course to take. They help us simplify[35] complicated
decisions for which we may never have all the information
to answer questions such as which apartment to rent or
whether to launch a Space Shuttle in the cold.

The pioneering work in the field of cognitive
heuristics is attributed to the winners of the 2002 Nobel
Prize in Economics, psychologists Daniel Kahneman
and Amos Tversky "for having integrated insights from
psychological research into economic science, especially
concerning human judgment and decision-making under
uncertainty"[36]. In his Nobel Prize Lecture[37] Kahneman
wrote "Our first joint article examined *systematic*[38] errors in
the casual statistical judgments of statistically sophisticated

---

[33] "Intuition becomes increasingly valuable in the new
information society precisely because there is so much data."
John Naisbitt

[34] "Life is the art of drawing sufficient conclusions from
insufficient premises." Samuel Butler.

[35] The role of heuristics in simplifying decisions is mirrored
in newspaper headlines where titles need to be short and
interesting. However, this guideline of short and interesting
can lead to misunderstanding such as "Miners refuse to work
after death", "Complaints about NBA growing ugly". Similarly
for the heuristics we will be describing. Context is important.

[36] http://www.econlib.org/library/Enc/bios/Kahneman.html

[37] (http://www.nobelprize.org/nobel_prizes/economicsciences
/laureates/2002/kahnemann-lecture.pdf

[38] Sytematic is the same as bias, that is, consistently erring on
the same side of a known value. This kind of error contrasts
with errors that occur randomly on both sides of the known
value. These unbiased errors, on the average, are close to
zero.   http://www.nobelprize.org/nobel_prizes/economics/
laureates/2002/kahnemann-lecture.pdf

researchers. Remarkably, the intuitive judgments of these experts did not conform to statistical principles with which they were thoroughly familiar . . . . we were impressed by the persistence of discrepancies between statistical intuition and statistical knowledge . . ."

This ". . . intuitive judgment . . ." leading to ". . . persistence of discrepancies . . ." is the crux of the problem we will be addressing. Statistical intuition: sometimes friend, sometimes foe.

Certain tasks may require more 'thought' (from the slow, rational system S2) than heuristics alone can provide, yet at times, when decisions have to be made on the fly, or when S2 is busy or resource challenged, the quick, intuitive S1 heuristics may be all that we have. The important thing is to be aware that these heuristics exist, so that proper precaution can be taken for their evaluation. This book is intended to both help us understand some of the limitations and errors in our intuitive thinking that allow subjective input to bias a decision, and also to identify some approaches that can be used to minimize these effects when suitable.

Getting positive results based on our use of heuristics when we successfully follow our hunches, our hearts, etc. can lead to reinforcement of our reliance on them.[39] This is sometimes, but not always, a good thing.[40] Since they enable simplification, reliance on heuristics often result in missing the devil in the details. I like to think of them as similar to the definition for epigrams of which Cervantes wrote, "They are short sentences drawn from long experience." Like epigrams, heuristics are quick (short) and generally

---

[39] Those who have the habit of revelation lose the habit of thought. Robin Skelton

[40] Historian Arnold Toynbee wrote, "Nothing fails [to continue improving] like success itself." Why change [a heuristic] if you have been successful in relying on it?"

provide adequate guidance learned from long, sometimes evolutionary, experience.[41] I think the following, attributed to Blaise Pascal, illustrates the idea that a heuristic develops with time/experience to hone or slough off unnecessary verbiage/qualifications in order to simplify a message/ decision: "I have made this letter longer than usual, only because I have not had the time to make it shorter" Blaise Pascal.

---

[41] Epigrams might generally contain good advice, but consider the following: Compare Sherlock Holmes' seemingly reasonable "It is a capital mistake to theorize before one has data." from Scandal in Bohemia, Sir Arthur Conan Doyle (1859-1930), with 'In the early 1800s, there was an ongoing scientific dispute as to whether or not it was possible to undertake a scientific study without some prior bias. Charles Darwin responded in a 1861 letter to a friend: "About thirty years ago there was much talk that geologists ought only to observe and not theorize; and I well remember someone saying that at this rate a man might as well go into a gravel-pit and count the pebbles and describe the colors. How odd it is that anyone should not see that all observation must be for or against some view if it is to be of any service."'—page 156 of Robert A. Burton's "On Being Certain". See also page 125 of Schulz book "Kuhn [author of the 1962 work, The Structure of Scientific Revolutions] challenged this notion [that scientists do not theorize until they have the evidence]—it is impossible to do science in the absence of a preexisting theory."

Truth be told, despite the apparent contradictions, both of these apparently contradictory philosophies have an element of truth. Blindly following either one can result in the dangerous simplification that heuristics can lead to, i.e., even though there is an element of truth in the adage, the context needs to be considered to understand when and where the heuristic has value. This kind of thinking is emphasized by Gigerenzer. He argues that when a heuristic leads to an incorrect bias, it may be that the environment in which the heuristic was employed is not appropriate for the environment in which the heuristic developed.

Two systems of thinking
S1 and S2

Our beliefs start with our sensory system, System 1. System 2[42] evaluates the feelings that S1 generates, mostly as an endorser, less often as the enforcer. System 2 may either justify or reject or simply give a "whatever . . .", letting S1 take over. S1 is generally associated with some of the evolutionarily older structures in the brain while S2 is associated with the pre-frontal cortex, what's up front. I use the vague concepts of both 'older structures' and 'associated with' to allow for all the rich diversity of connections that underlie the processes of thought, learning, and memory built with 80 billion neurons and 10 trillion synapses.

The operations of System 1 [intuitive, S1] are fast, automatic, effortless, associative and difficult to control or modify. The operations of System 2 [rational, S2] are slower, serial, effortful, and deliberately controlled. System 1 is involved in translating what it senses into the emotions/feelings that S2 can apply to its judgments. The rational mind can sometimes filter and process input from S1. If S2 is not diligent, impressions from the subconscious can lead to a false judgment, a triumph of the rash over the rational.

It's an uncomfortable feeling to contemplate that our actions are dominated by the unconscious S1 that, by definition, we are not conscious of. Along the same lines, Gladwell wrote:

"I think we are innately suspicious of this kind of rapid cognition [a rapid assessment by S1]. We live in a world that assumes that the quality of a decision is directly related to the time and effort that went into making it. When doctors

---

[42]   K2011 pg 20. "I adopt terms originally proposed by the psychologists Keith Stanovich and Richard West, and will refer to two systems in the mind, System 1 and System 2."

are faced with a difficult diagnosis, they order more tests, and when we are uncertain about what we hear, we ask for a second opinion. And what do we tell our children? Haste makes waste. Look before you leap. Stop and think. Don't judge a book by its cover. We believe that we are always better off gathering as much information as possible and spending as much time as possible in deliberation."[43] Despite this common advice to search for complete information, we will later see how a hospital improved its efficiency and efficacy by using less information to classify patients entering the ER. Other examples will show how intuition can give a quick and accurate response when S2 can't.

From Taleb, "It is a fact that our brain tends to go for superficial clues when it comes to risk and probability, these clues being largely determined by what emotions they elicit or the ease with which they come to mind. In addition to such problems with the perception of risk, it is also a scientific fact, and a shocking one, that both risk detection and risk avoidance are not mediated in the "thinking" part of the brain but largely in the emotional one (the "risk as feelings" theory). The consequences are not trivial: It means that rational thinking has little, very little, to do with risk avoidance. Much of what rational thinking seems to do is rationalize one's action by fitting some logic to them."[44]

How our assessments of risk have a large emotional content is covered later in this book. We will see that for the sake of cohesiveness, we link benefits and risks inversely so that when given accounts of the benefits of making a certain decision, we not only make a more positive evaluation of the benefits, but also, for consistency, evaluate the risks as less risky.

---

[43]   Blink pg 13
[44]   Taleb Black pg 38

Another factor in determining the likelihood or frequency of an event is the availability, or ease with which it comes to mind. The Availability Heuristic leads us to believe the easier an incident is imagined, the more frequently it occurs. The next chapter goes into some detail as to why factors such as salience and presentation (framing) of the question can bias this rule of thumb. Taleb's comment on the influence of emotion is tied to the Affect Heuristic where we unconsciously substitute an emotional question for the original question. Asked 'which is the best car', we substitute, 'which car do I like more'. Taleb's final comments on where decisions of risk are made, speaks to our hunches, our intuitions, our feelings, that pertain to the workings of System 1 that is quicker to the punch every time than the rational mind (S2). The task for the rational mind is to make up stories that are consistent with our feelings, or else to explain why we should not accept them. This role of S2 assumes there is a window of opportunity to act. When the S2 is stressed out, it may not have the desire to get involved in another evaluation. Let's look at some examples that illustrate this point.

System 2 availability

Our rational minds are lazy and want to be in a state of cognitive ease according to Kahneman[45]. I would say the mind like to get comfortable, and that means not being

---

[45] K2011 pg 121. "People adjust less (stay closer to the anchor) when their mental resources are depleted, either because their memory is loaded with digits or because they are slightly drunk. Insufficient adjustment is a failure of a weak or lazy System2." Kahneman argues (2011, pg 35) for the law of least effort (Much as Occam's razor chooses the simplest solution) which instructs us that in general, we do the least amount of work necessary to resolve an issue, to decide what to believe.

challenged with an overload of problems. Tiredness and
hunger are physical considerations that can test and deplete
the rational mind's reserves of mental energy. As well,
mental exertion such as having to remember a multi-digit
number while performing another task, or paying attention
to an ambiguous problem[46] can tap the mental budget.
When S2 is tanked, we rely more on S1 and all its rules of
thumb, its heuristics, its biases.

When you are physically tired System 2 will adjust
less from an anchor[47] because it takes extra work at
each adjustment, and each decision lowers your energy
reserves. The first adjustment when you are rested and
nourished may seem easy compared to future additional
justifications.[48] Since we have a bias to believe, and the
anchor is less easily challenged when stressed, our tendency
is to not change, to not adjust, to accept weak arguments as
truth. Picture the Snicker commercials where the body has
apparently been deprived of glucose. "You're not yourself"
(until you've had a Snicker). The question of how fatigue
affects the strengthening of an anchor is addressed in the
following studies.

In one experiment,[49] participants were shown a
nonsense word followed by "true" or "false". When the S2
was occupied with maintaining a multi-digit number in
mind, participants recalled many of the false couplings as
true. We are biased to believe, and if this bias is not kept
in check by a rested S2, we will be prone to too readily
accepting falsehoods as truths in our story building. See
Chapter 5 for a discussion of the concept of stories. For

---

[46]   SCIAM Mind May / June 2013
[47]   K2011 pg 119 ". . . an anchoring effect occurs when people
        consider a particularly irrelevant value for an unknown
        quantity before estimating that quantity." Though logically
        irrelevant, anchoring has an effect on the quantity's estimate.
[48]   K2011 pg 121
[49]   K2011 pg 81

now, stories can be thought of models to help explain and justify our thoughts and actions.

In another experiment[50] that further demonstrates the laziness of S2, called the MPG Illusion, a question of money saved depending on changes to gas use efficiency was posed:

Adam switches from a gas-guzzler of 12 mpg to a slightly less voracious guzzler that runs at 14 mpg.

The environmentally virtuous Beth switches from a 30 mpg car to one that runs at 40 mpg.

If they each run their cars 10,000 miles, who will save more by switching? My first lazy thought was that this was a no-brainer, Beth's change seemed much more positive. My lazy S2 didn't do the math, it seemed that obvious. The reason that this is called the MPG Illusion is that Adam saves more than Beth. The solution is that he will lower his use from 833 (12mpg into 10,000 miles) to 714 gallons (14 into 10,000), while Beth's usage will drop from 333 to 250.

A worrisome observation on how judges deny requests for parole based on how hungry they are.

"A disturbing demonstration of depletion effects in judgment was recently reported in the Proceedings of the National Academy of Sciences. The unwitting participants in the study were eight parole judges in Israel. They spend entire days reviewing applications for parole. The cases are presented in random order, and the judges spend little time on each one, an average of 6 minutes. (The default decision is denial of parole; only 35% of requests are approved. The exact time of each decision is recorded, and the times of the judges' three food breaks—morning break, lunch, and afternoon break-during the day are recorded as well.) The authors of the study plotted the proportion of approved requests against the time since the last food break. The proportion spikes after each meal, when about 65% of

---

50 K2011 pg 372

requests are granted. During the two hours or so until the judges' next feeding, the approval rate drops steadily, to about zero just before the meal. As you might expect, this is an unwelcome result and the authors carefully checked many alternative explanations. The best possible account of the data provides bad news: tired and hungry judges tend to fall back on the easier default position of denying request for parole. Both fatigue and hunger probably play a role."[51]

It is worthwhile to remember that S1 is a real time system that is focused in the moment by moment that S2 usually has no reason to react to. Unless S1 senses a sharp change in sensory input that sets the organism on a fight or flight response, it will pass along a bland story that there is nothing to worry about.

From Kahneman 2011 pg 81 ". . . when System 2 is otherwise engaged, we will believe almost anything. System 1 is gullible and biased to believe, System 2 is in charge of doubting and unbelieving, but System2 is sometimes busy, and often lazy. Indeed, there is evidence that people are more likely to be influenced by empty persuasive messages, such as commercials, when they are tired and depleted."

---

[51]   In the Lilienfield Jan/Feb 2013 SA Mind article, "In 1990 psychologist Daniel Gilbert, now at Harvard University, and his co-authors presented participants with statements based on a word from the Hopi language (such as "a monischa is an armadillo") a few seconds later participants learned whether the assertion was true or false. Subjects were distracted in the intervening seconds by a challenging task—hitting a button as soon as they heard a musical tone—intended to prevent them from processing these statements mentally and, in effect, shutting down System 2. Later, when Gilbert asked distracted subjects whether each statement was true or false, they were more likely to identify the statements as true. Believing is our default state, it comes to us naturally, disbelieving does not."

If you don't know the answer to the question, change the question.

"This is the essence of intuitive heuristics: when faced with a difficult question, we often answer an easier one instead, usually without noticing the substitution."[52]

For example, the Availability Heuristic equates ease of remembering or ease of constructing a concept as a measure of how common or frequent the concept is. If it's easy to recall, it's probably commonly occurring. If you are asked for the actor who has made the most movies in the last 20 years, you may subconsciously answer an easier question[53], such as, 'which actor has made the most movies in the last few years?' or your memory may go straight to famous actors or your personal favorite since you are familiar with their work and you are less likely to forget their lesser movies than those of another actor. A supporting actor may have frequent unimportant parts in many movies, but isn't easily brought to mind, so he is considered (wrongly, but in agreement with this Availability Heuristic) to have not made many movies.

Altering these questions may not be right, but it's also probably not far wrong. Your Availability Heuristic gave you a quick, reasonable answer consistent with the question. While the error in this 'Who is the actor'? is probably not critical—close will usually do, there are situations where a more structured (S2 thinking) process should be called on. A tool for calculating relative risks, called FMEA (see glossary) used in the process of risk analysis, requires estimates of severity, frequency of occurrence, and ability to detect a given failure in order to rank its priority in developing safeguards and ranking for resource allowance. When biased mental measures are used to estimate these

---

[52] K2011 pg 12
[53] K2011 pg 13

variables, the result could prove costly. Perhaps a recent critical equipment failure may fool your mind into thinking that that kind of failure is common, just because it was easy to recall. Or, a recently attended seminar on process maintenance might have you thinking that an equipment failure was due to a calibration error, just because it was included in the meeting and came to mind effortlessly. Again, this is your unconscious availability heuristic applying an unfortunate bias to your frequency estimate based on ease of recall. You consciously make your decision without realizing this heuristic had already made the call for you. Your conscious 'decision' is really more of a conscious test of agreement of S2 with the S1 call.

As much as we try to minimize the subjective aspects of decision making, we will soon see that this is not an easy task. The quotes at the beginning of the chapter credited to Hein and Burton touch on the issue of what we think we know. Researchers have demonstrated that based on our falsely elevated levels of confidence, we know less than we think we do and we 'don't know what we knowest not'.[54] For unconscious knowledge (gut feelings), we may unconsciously know more than we consciously think we know as seen in the following.

Individuals with prosopagnosia have difficulty recognizing faces. According to US Weekly[55] Brad Pitt thinks he may have this condition. Studies have shown that a person with this condition can have a normal visual sensation and be able to describe a face, but are unable to put it all together to achieve face recognition. However, if

---

[54]   Taleb Black pg 147 "You cannot ignore self-delusion. The problem with [false] experts is that they do not know what they do not know." True experts do.

[55]   May 22, 2013 http://www.usmagazine.com/celebrity-news/news/brad-pitt-says-he-cant-remember-faces-thinks-he-suffers-from-prosopagnosia-2013225

the face is of a loved one, "Their autonomic nervous system responds with measureable perspiration and speeded pulse. What the conscious mind cannot understand, the heart knows."[56]

In another example of our limited awareness of our perceptions, when an object is flashed to a subject's right brain, they cannot describe what they saw. When asked to use their left hand to feel around a number of hidden objects for the one that had been flashed, they had no difficulty finding the correct object. They picked out the correct one easily. Out of sight out of mind? Not exactly.

Subjects were exposed to a very brief scene that was either emotionally positive or negative. Due to the short exposure, subjects only perceived these scenes as a flash, yet they had the effect of influencing the pictures of people shown after the flash. "People somehow looked nicer if their photo immediately followed unperceived kittens rather than an unperceived werewolf."[57]

Intuition

These gut level, intuitive, S1 mental rules of thumb have survived in our neural processes because they work quickly and quietly, generally leading to adequate decisions, helping us avoid analysis paralysis.[58] These shortcuts are powerful in part because we are generally unaware of their

---

[56] Myers pg 5

[57] Myers pg 27

[58] See the classic story of Buridan's ass that dies of starvation because he can't decide (analysis paralysis) between two sources of food between which he's located. On the other hand, too much reliance on feelings to get to a quick resolution to an ambiguous situation can lead to ignoring important information. For example, a strongly held opinion may have made sense in the past, but a changed context might require

existence. As an example of the power of intuitive thinking, Gladwell shares a story in his book, Blink. In 1983, an art dealer had an ancient statue known as a 'kouros', of which there are only about 200 in the world, most of which were in much worse condition than his. He was asking $10 million. The authenticity of the work was supported by some historical documents and consistency with other pieces of that period. The statue was analyzed in great detail using state of the art analytical equipment. One finding was that the statue was covered with a thin layer of calcite, a process which may take hundreds if not thousands of years to form. After more than a year of study, the J. Paul Getty Museum bought it. Its first public showing was announced on the front page of the NY Times. Despite all of this analysis, a number of art experts 'felt' that something was wrong. For one of these experts the first thought that came into his head was 'fresh', not quite what you might think would be appropriate for such an ancient item that had spent so much time buried in the earth. A consensus was growing that the kouros was not authentic. For one expert, his first look at it gave him a sense of "intuitive repulsion". This statue was too far from his expectations of his model of what a kouros should look like. It was as if his boat was rocked and nausea from a fluctuating horizon had set in. Meanwhile, another geologist concluded that the calcite covering could have been created using a potato mold for a couple of months.

The intuitions of these experts had outperformed the analyses from a team of scientists. This integrative ability of intuition was able to apply, somewhat unconsciously, all of its knowledge in a New York second.

Everything should be made as simple as possible, but not more so. Einstein

---

a re-evaluation. In such a situation we need to "scrub off our assumptions" and this extra work is not welcome.

'Don't sweat the small stuff', and 'it's almost all small stuff', seem to be a simplifying default principle of System 1.

In our need for speed, heuristics occasionally prevail over Albert's advice. We expect simplification in the solutions and decisions that most heuristics provide. From H. L. Mencken, *The Divine Afflatus*, "For every complex problem there is a solution that is simple, neat, and wrong." While simplification is part and parcel of a fast and frugal decision making process, it can lead to neglect of some critical details.[59] For example, suppose you are trying to determine the variability of a process. One simplification might be to not consider the effect of variability contributed by the measurement system. If the measurement adds no variation to the value, the simplification is worthwhile. On the contrary, if the measurement system was responsible for 50% of the final variation, ignoring it would be a bad idea. If this information about relative contributions of variation is not available, don't assume perfect measurements. This simplification heuristic[60] points us in the right direction, but for decisions that matter, we must first acquire knowledge. We need to learn what it is that we do not know, so that we can simplify with better justification.

When a value is presented that appears to have few significant digits, a heuristic based reaction may make you think that little is known about this number. An imprecise number may appear more of a guess than a measurement. If I say there are 1000 marbles in the jar, don't you wonder if that number is exactly true, or its use was meant to confer some reasonable degree of uncertainty, like 'more or less 5'

---

[59] William Thompson, Lord Kelvin wrote "The more you understand what is wrong with a figure, the more valuable that figure becomes." Understanding "What's wrong" here translates into understanding the factors that contribute to total variability, both of the process and its measurement.

[60] See Occam's Razor

marbles? If I say there are 1001 marbles in the jar, would that give you a little more confidence as to this number's reliability? This play of presentation with precision will influence the range of values for which you are able to adjust your answer away from, the anchor. Without knowing the process that provided values of 1000 or 1001, I would guess the 1000 would have a range of something like plus or minus between +/-5 and +/-50. For the 1001, I'm guessing plus or minus between 0 and 5, but that's just me. As an anchor, the number 1000 allows greater liberty than 1001 in determining how far from it we are willing to adjust our estimate of its true value. In other words, an anchor low in precision has greater ability to influence estimates than one with more precise values.[61] In risk management, we don't want decisions to be made based on false understanding of the reliability of a number. Don't assume flawless measurements. Don't assume your number is 'the' number. Get the precision appropriate to the purpose of the problem. Understanding your process includes understanding the measurements of that process and how and for what those values will be used.[62]

A tool as useful as a control chart relies on data with sufficient resolution (precision) to allow it to do its job of detecting trends or other out of control signals. Grind off the precision enough and you have a flat line in more ways than one. Appropriate precision comes from knowing when to fold them and when to hold them, when to reveal and when to conceal. Holding on to too much precision gives the impression of knowledge greater than it is. On a visit to the Bayamon Puerto Rico Science Park, I remember

---

[61]   With simplification as an S1 M.O., I have seen numbers get rounded to less precise values, sometime to the point that they are little more than useless.

[62]   There is nothing worse than a sharp image of a fuzzy concept. Ansel Adams

reading a plaque stating that an artifact was 1006 years old. I immediately wondered if that value was updated yearly. No doubt we would better understand this value if the original figure was presented with some sense of a range of values that were most likely distributed around the 1006 figure. A plus or minus, like 1006 +/-15 might give a better feeling for the accuracy of the value. If 1006 was a known value and not an estimate, that should be communicated.

"Knowing what thou knowest not" could be rephrased to 'estimating how good the precision is, comes from knowing how much we don't know about a number.' If we know what we don't know about a figure, we will be more knowledgeable in using that number as the point from which to make adjustments in our estimate of the true value. The less we know what we don't know about a number, the less confidence we should have, and so should increase the size of confidence intervals around the estimated point value.

When the solution is simple, God is answering. A. Einstein

Bear in a Bush

Heuristics have evolutionary roots where they once helped us to simplify swift decision making in order to react and avoid the dangers and pursue the opportunities of the day. I will use the 'bear in a bush' scenario from time to time to illustrate how, like our ancestors, we continue to need to decide between the extremes of (A) being too conservative in trying to avoid all danger or (B) being too fearlessly adventurous or (C) by following more nuanced responses in reaction to the environmental context.

The bear in a bush problem, as do many decision making scenarios, presents two kinds of errors, imaginatively named Type 1 and Type 2. Type 1 error occurs when you think there is a bear in the bush but there isn't, and Type 2 error occurs when you don't think there is a bear, but there is. We will look at this in more detail when we indicate the effect of biased heuristics and when we talk about which kind of error is tolerable, and which less so. Generally speaking, if you reduce the probability of one of these kinds of errors, you will increase the likelihood of the other.

Approaches A and B (see above) are associated with the hedgehog whose reaction to most problems is typically to roll up into a ball of spiny protrusions, while decision C is more associated with the fox who has various options within reach. The philosopher Isaiah Berlin wrote[63] of a Greek saying, "The fox knows many things, but the hedgehog knows one big thing" . . . when in doubt, roll up into a ball of defensive spines. The fox's approach leads to learning while lowering the chance of the accompanying indecision or wrong calls that could get him killed.[64] In the next section we will see an approach to risk analysis that will help us begin to think in more detail about error control. First, a few heuristic examples to help get a feel of when their simplifications work, and when not so much.

Sometimes it's right to be wrong. Consider the following heuristic rule. Certainly an elevated concern is more warranted for animals or foreign tribes approaching than receding from us. Sounds that are coming toward us are perceived as closer and louder than they really are, while the opposite is true for receding sounds. This is a bias that has a perfectly good explanation. Approaching objects are

---

[63]   Lehrer pg 241

[64]   The old chestnut here is that ships are safe when they are in harbor, but that is not what they are built for. Some risks, including those that are associated with keeping the status quo, are inevitable.

inherently more dangerous than are receding ones—hence the value of earlier and more acute detection of them to take the prudent action.

Another heuristic tells us that an object's distance can be estimated by how visually well defined it appears. Blurred images appear farther away. This estimation of distance based on clarity may be generally reliable but less so when a fog sets in.

Yet another heuristic nudges us to judge a precipice's height as higher when observed from above than from below. You are safe at the base, so your estimate will not be affected by fear. Better safe than sorry is consistent with the asymmetric consequences of failed prediction depending on where you are looking from, your point of view, the context. From the top of a tree, the drop to the ground looks much farther that does the same distance viewed from the ground.

Our behavior is influenced by our intuitive understanding of probability. We will see several more examples where a quick estimate of an event's frequency will be biased by our unconscious heuristics. For an example of inappropriate behavior based on a misunderstanding of basic regression statistics, Kahneman presents the problem of the practice of rewarding an excellent performance or punishing a bad one[65]. If a person has a certain average performance, then exceptional performance, whether good or bad, is by definition at or beyond the expected range of results for that person. Following an exceptional performance, regardless of whether or not punishment or reward or nothing is applied, will be a performance probably closer to the average (regression to the mean) than the current exceptional performance. So, a poor performance will appear to be improved by punishment, and a good

---

[65]   K+T pg 10

performance will appear to worsen by reward. This will lead to the conclusion that punishment works better than rewards. The ancients understood this situation: "There is in the worst of fortune the best of chances for a happy change." (and vice versa) Euripides

I hope that these few examples gave you a sense of the value of judgments that are biased to protect us in some situations, yet appear like errors of reason in others. Context is critical.

Pauling, Patterns, and Predictions

In the opening scene of the movie A Beautiful Mind, the brilliant mathematician John Nash gets a little lost in thought while contemplating the pattern on a fellow student's tie, and declares "There has to be a mathematical explanation for how bad that tie is." One thing that we do constantly and unconsciously is to look for patterns of cause and effect. We don't like to be left hanging with an incomplete story. We, like Nash, want closure, an explanation, an equation. What we don't do well is ambiguity. This predisposition for pattern assignment is so strong that we are more likely to assign, for example, size differences between two groups of sticks, where either none or little exist, just by labeling them 'A' and 'B'. The decision to err on the side of Type 1 error, false alarms, is strongly enabled by the need to find patterns, to avoid the anxiety of ambiguity. This need for closure pushes us into believing things that just aren't so, but it also is a necessary consequence of our evolutionary progress. Let's see how heuristics help make this happen.

Gigerenzer makes the argument quite nicely that evolution has equipped us with brains that continually hypothesize, model, or seek to find patterns[66] that explain what's going on around us. Here's the bear in the bush problem again where a rustling in the leaves could be nothing to be alarmed at, just a breeze passing through, or it could be a bear. When faced with the rustle we must react quickly. We have a choice that, broadly worded, is between being alarmed and not being alarmed. In either case, if we are correct, we have practically no cost associated with our decisions. We were either correct in predicting a bear that is actually there and took steps to avoid it, or we were correct in predicting no bear. If we failed, we either predicted a bear that's not there (type 1 error, false alarm) or we predicted no bear when there was one (type 2 error, no alarm). A role of evolution has been to determine the relative costs of these two kinds of errors, the falsely alarmed and the falsely unconcerned. Type 1 errors come from inappropriate action, Type 2 from inappropriate inaction. It is sometimes said that the two kinds of error are divided between those who thought and never did and those who did and never thought.[67]

As Winston Churchill is purported to have said: "When I look back on all these worries I remember the story of the old man who said on his deathbed that he had had a lot of trouble in his life, most of which had never happened." False alarms are an affordable cost, the unnecessary worry for the trouble that never happened.

In order to err on the side of more generally less costly false alarms, evolution has equipped us to look for and posit all kinds of connections, the better to find more true

---

[66]   In statistics, apophenia (the condition of seeing patterns that aren't there, false alarms.) is known as a Type I error

[67]   Another way of thinking about these errors is to separate them into of actions, (commission), or inaction (omission).

relationships of cause and effect.[68] As twice Nobel Laureate Linus Pauling said: "The best way to have a good idea is to have a lot of ideas."[69]

This need to make sense out of events for which we have limited information, motivates us to unconsciously make rules (heuristics), and rules about rules, or 'meta-rules'. The result of learning from our mistakes of following the rules that were wrong is that these rules should get changed or adjusted for changes in context. This, we are told, is what smart people do. Learning this from the action of others, is what wise people do. Preventing the problem altogether is what geniuses do, if Einstein is to be believed.

One aspect of the ability to prevent problems is derived from our ability to predict. Daniel Gilbert, professor of psychology at Harvard University, wrote in the 07-02-2006 Los Angeles Times: "The brain is a beautifully engineered get-out-the-way machine that constantly scans the environment for things out of whose way it should right now get. That's what brains did for several hundred million years—and then, just a few million years ago, the mammalian brain learned a new trick: to predict the timing and location of dangers before they actually happened."

Our ability to predict, to accurately simulate the future, relies upon bias-resistant thinking in order to obtain valid results. To this end, heuristics are intrinsically interesting because they contaminate our thinking by promoting biased simplifications of the judgment and decision making process. This bias was probably quite adaptive for

---

[68]   Shermer pg 62 "Because we must make associations in order to survive and reproduce, natural selection favored all association-making strategies, even those that resulted in false positives."

[69]   The consequence of coming up with a lot of ideas is the need to winnow out the bad ones. With all these ideas being formed, "We are trying to prove ourselves wrong as quickly as possible, because only in that way can we find progress." Feynman

the Flintstones, but not always so much these days where encounters with bears are not quite a daily concern. We need to be aware of these biases to avoid or calibrate their influence in important decisions such as whether the weather is warm enough to launch a Challenger shuttle.

First impressions and stereotypes

Stereotypes are made from deduction of the individual from the general while induction is to infer, to divine the general from the individual. We overplay the latter, and underplay the former.

They say you never get a second chance to make a first impression. Just as we are unable to undo an optical illusion even when we know what the truth is, it's very difficult to undo first impressions or stereotyping[70]. First impressions

---

[70] We can stretch the usual effect of first impressions and stereotyping to include the Halo Effect. All of these heuristics rely on our need to add congruent information to an incomplete understanding, and all understanding is incomplete. Our first impression is a sample, and usually a biased one at that. We intuitively know how important that first impression is, and we try a little extra to make it a good one. When we have to make a decision on an outlier from sample intensive practices such as PAT (Process Analytical Technology), do we just throw out the result as being non-informative, an isolated event, or do we fully investigate? The answer might reside in a past experience. Do we stereotype the problem? ('We've seen this before, don't worry about it.') Do we halo effect it by making it a bigger problem? ('I never trusted this process, let's give this a thorough review.') When we review a quality process do we assume safety and efficacy? ('We never had problems with safety here before, and nothing has changed, so . . .'). When we chose a sample size for a DOE, do we use the minimal sampling and testing assuming this is just a confirmatory step, or do we use a sample size that addresses the vigilance needed to keep the process in control? Our decisions can be influenced by our

are lasting and may grow stronger over time even without additional supporting evidence, so it's important to derive this initial judgment relatively free from bias. First impressions influenced by stereotypes associated with a group become delusional when they are assumed to apply to everyone in the group.

We unconsciously tend to size up someone we have just met for the first time by filling in (Nature hates a vacuum.) missing information about them based on simplifications and assumptions. Often a stereotype comes to mind that supplies the missing information. Upon meeting someone new, we may ask 'What do her clothes, accent, or demeanor suggest to us? Do they fit a pattern that may predict other more important characteristics?' Suppose she doesn't speak English very well. You know some folks that haven't had a good opportunity to learn a lot of English due to factors beyond their control, such as where they were raised. Does this person we have just met fit the stereotype of having come from poor conditions or had hard times earlier in life? Is she from another country where English is not the first language? Do her clothes provide a hint? (Frank Zappa would ask,[71] "Is that a real poncho . . . I mean Is that a Mexican poncho or is that a Sears poncho?"). How about the car she arrived in or the people she is seen with? The subconscious runs the gauntlet in a flash to decide what associations make a cohesive fit with the known. It turns out that this first, thinly sliced impression is adequate if not better (because it is focused on what matters, little

---

first impressions and need to act accordingly. When deciding on a sampling plan for risk analysis, do we assume homogeneity (promoting the delusion that 'they' are all alike) and make a convenience (a.k.a. grab or opportunity) sample, or do we assume heterogeneity and take a representative sample to challenge the homogeneity assumption? Play it safe, assume heterogeneity, take the risk of a false alarm.

[71]   The song Camarillo Brillo from the record Overnight Sensation

influenced by irrelevant information) than a post first impression determination.

Stereotypes are easier to remember than all the details they shelter. "Stereotypes are particular kinds of expectations that can function to guide and shape reality, and they may do so, at least in part, through an availability bias. Hamilton and Rose (1978) explored this possibility in their stereotyping research. In one study, subjects were given lists of sentences of the form, "Carol, a librarian, is attractive and serious." In each of the sentences, a member of an occupation was described as possessing two traits. Some of the traits bore a stereotypic association to the occupation as, for example, in the case of the trait "serious," with the occupation "librarian"; in other cases the traits were non-stereotypic for that occupation. However, when subjects were asked to estimate the number of times each trait had described a member of each occupation, they misremembered the trait-occupation pairings to favor stereotypical associations. For example, they were more likely to remember librarians had been serious than that waitresses had been serious. Here we have a bias, the Availability Heuristic, which has eased the recalling of pre-established conceptions, stereotypes.[72]

"Many stereotypes permit the economy of expression necessary for rapid communication and effective functioning."[73] Probably not all DMVs should have a sign that says "Abandon hope all ye who enter here" but the message may still be generally applicable enough that you are prepared for a day of frustration when you have to go there. Believing a lie is sometimes the rational way to maintain your sanity.

An unfortunate result of relying on stereotypes is that having linked a certain stereotypical behavior with a person,

---

[72] K + T pg 198
[73] Paulos pg 28

we may be lead to assume that the behavior has actually been displayed by him. For example, let's say a few salient individuals belonging to a group were somewhat obnoxious, and evidence of similar behavior was noticed in some other group members. Another member, of whom nothing is known except that he is a member of the group, might be charged with having committed this same behavior, just because he was a member of the group.

The Halo effect

"The tendency to like (or dislike) everything about a person—including things you have not observed—is known as the halo effect . . . It is one of the ways the representation of the world that System 1 generates is simpler and more coherent than the real thing."[74]

While the halo effect is usually used to refer to positive characteristics, it doesn't rule out less angelic attributes. The Halo effect is simply the assumption of unknown characteristics being consistent with other known ones. It is the individualization of stereotyping. Instead of assigning attributes to a person consistent with the crowd they run with, the halo effect attributes are assigned based on consistency with other characteristics of that same person. For example, a well groomed, intelligent child who has excellent manners might also be expected to not be a prankster. Once we are primed by his good manners, it is easier to think of him being nice than to think of him as a mischievous individual.[75] Examples from TV shows with exceptions to this 'rule' include Leave it to Beaver's

---

[74]   K2011 pg82
[75]   Baron pg 193 "If a teacher thinks that a child is intelligent, she will also tend to rate this student as well behaved, even if the child is no better behaved than average."

Eddie Haskell who comes to mind as being surprisingly duplicitous in his behavior. Perhaps a more recent example like The Office's Jim Halpert is more accessible. Ok, how about Modern Family's Luke?

The Halo Effect is our mind's way of assigning compatible characteristics to complete someone we already know something about. We have models about the world that we try to stand by. When we experience an uncomfortable feeling of uncertainty in these models, we confabulate the missing information with coherent and cohesive guesses. The rule of the Halo effect is that the person or model we are completing is made consistent with what is already known of that person, sometimes our first impressions. This practice is biased even further if the person is also stereotyped. Because we perceive a person as thin, doesn't imply that she goes to the gym often, but the two descriptions are consistent with each other and with our model that ties together appearances and possible reasons for them.

An example[76] of this heuristic at work asks, based on the following descriptors, who do you like best? Read the descriptors quickly, just once.

Alan: intelligent—industrious—impulsive—critical—stubborn—envious

Ben: envious—stubborn—critical—impulsive—industrious—intelligent

In a job interview where the two candidates use these self descriptive adjectives, studies have shown that interviewers stop listening after the first few. The lesson here might be to first put your best foot forward. It may also serve as a reminder to look at a problem from different viewpoints.

---

[76]   K2011pg82

In this job interview Framing, how the information was presented, is another cognitive bias that shouldn't affect a decision, but it does. Framing often answers the question with the question. Anchoring shares at least one characteristic with framing in that they both can subconsciously bias and steer the answers of responders.

The following is one of my favorite passages from "The Halo Effect"[77]:

> "Bill George, former CEO of Medtronic, advanced a similar list about leadership in his 2003 book, Authentic Leadership: Rediscovering the Secrets of Creating Lasting Value. George wrote that outstanding leaders share a handful of qualities, including steadfast courage, clear vision, personal integrity, and outstanding character. They are authentic leaders. Not surprisingly, all the examples came from successful companies. George also mentioned a handful of failed companies, and their leaders were always inauthentic. Well, you can always find good things to say about leaders at successful companies, and you can always find reasons to criticize leaders of failing firms. A critical reader ought to ask if any successful companies have inauthentic leaders, and if any unsuccessful companies are run by authentic leaders, because if not, it's quite possible we're just throwing around Halos."

Our need for consistency here affects our opinions. A good leader in a bad company is harder to accept than a bad leader in a bad company.

---

[77]   Rosenzweig, pg 58

When a company is doing well, praise is heaped on management which is tied to the need to have a believable story of cause and effect. While management might have been known for some good characteristics such as being 'people persons', and other traits such as being innovative and risk taking, all this may get turned on its head when the company goes through some hard times. Now the manager was too innovative, did not stick with tried and true practices. He took too many risks. The managers didn't change, but in trying to tell a good story, their characteristics had to change with the changing fortunes of their companies. The Halo must remain consistent with context, and so is subject to twist with shifting conditions. We create consistency, and performance is what we want to be consistent with. As goes the company's performance, so go the perceived characteristics of its leader.

To remain constant, things must change.

If we have leaders we trust, that may lead, by way of the Halo Effect, to too much confidence in them. We may assume that f they got X right, they're probably correct on Y as well. On the other hand, if we disagree strongly on some issue important to both of us, I might assume that we will not agree on other issues either.

In the chapter on storytelling we will see how important it is for us to resolve doubt. Fitting missing information that is consistent with known information and beliefs is a way to reduce that uncomfortable uncertainty.

Group think[78] the social animal

Yet another decision making bias to add to the list, Group Think can be a powerful and negative influence on decisions related to change. Suffer not doubt; your charismatic leader has already voiced his opinion. No doubt is no problem so don't you dare shake the boat. The group needs to present a united front. Be a team player. Peer pressure predominates, and we elevate our level of confidence to fit an environment where we have effectively passed personal responsibility to the group and/or its leader. Groupthink leads to the illusion of unanimity (no one is dissenting, we must all be in agreement, our decisions have the appearance of wide spread agreement) which leads to overconfidence and risky behavior.

Those that dissent, whether of an out-group or not, are considered biased on the question at hand, and by what I call the twisted halo effect, the person who has contradictory opinions is not only wrong on this particular question, he's probably considered wrong on anything else that the group is proposing. As well, when circumstances occur that challenge our thoughts and opinions of a person, the halo changes, or twists, to accommodate an altered set of circumstances. The bias to look only for confirmatory evidence is multiplied in the groupthink setting. Cognitive ease appears when dissention is self-censored. We're in with the in crowd on the bandwagon of false consensus.

---

[78] Paulospg 49, referring to the work of Irvin Janis on the interactions of members in a group . . . "Since members wish to be valued by the group, they freely express opinions in line with what they perceive to be the group's attitudes and suppress views that run counter to those of the group. A self-reinforcing, prejudicial breeze soon kicks up. Leaders arise who are more extreme than the average member; they typically pick yes-men rather than more independent-minded members and are deferred to by most others—particularly if said leader can influence the latter's careers."

Instinctive conformity (mimicry) and rationalized conformity (organizational).

Under the heading of **Instinctive conformity** we find the ancestral roots of our brain's hard wiring[79] to link our behavior to our need to distinguish and belong to our family, our tribe. One of the most famous examples of mimicry is from the work of anthropologist Konrad Lorenz who found that graylag geese would imprint on whatever was available in the thirteen to sixteen hour period after they hatched. In one experiment, they imprinted on Lorenz's boots and would follow him around as if he were their mother. Geese that do not possess this early drive and behavior to join their family probably had associated survival issues and contributed less to geese's current behavior.

The advantages of being part of the group leads us to display signs of identity with the group such as through mimicry. Yawning in response to another's yawn is an example of a signal we unconsciously send to others to demonstrate our identity with them. This is just one of many ways heuristics influence our behavior. In a similar way, some of us change our accent and grammatical style to mimic the audience we are talking with. Emotions, such as happiness, can be contagious and also link strangers. Some humorous beer commercials taken place at sports bars play on this, usually male, bonding when the home team does well.

A more recent example of instinctive conformity comes from work on mirror neurons. This type of neuron is at

---

[79] As an example of our ability to vicariously experience an activity, experiments with monkeys show that increased brain activity was virtually the same whether the monkey was actually mimicking an action or just watching the action. Monkey see, monkey do, if only in their minds. Herbert page 68

work when a human sees someone doing something that he has had experience with. We find these neurons activating much as they do in the observer as in the actual doers. Our susceptibility to this desire seems to be associated with our level of empathy.[80] More empathetic individuals appear to be more capable of mentally 'connecting' with another's activity. The parts of the brain that activate when I throw a ball are the same parts that activate when I watch someone else throw a ball. The dark side of this empathetic attitude is that 'cheaters' can take advantage of this feeling. Disalvo warns us not to be so empathetic with used car salesmen or anyone else for whom our crude B.S. detectors have been deactivated by empathy and cannot save us from being duped.

rationalized conformity (organizations)

We go along to get along.[81] This is particularly appropriate for military and religious organizations. While instinctive conformity is an unconscious activity, rationalized conformity is closer to what we think when we think about the purposeful conformity of organizations. I define purposeful here as what the group needs, not necessarily what the individual wants. Group think is at work when there is pressure to not dissent, nor even to bring other considerations to the table. As the group matures, this 'understanding' becomes further entrenched.

---

[80]   They say that to get know someone before you criticize them, first walk a mile in their shoes. That way, when you do criticize them, you're a mile away and have their shoes.

[81]   K2011 pg 209 "For some of our most important beliefs we have no evidence at all, except that people we love and trust hold these beliefs." Schulz pg 133 "Our faith is faith in someone else's faith, and in the greatest matters this is most the case." (William James, "The Will to Believe")

Creativity is not cultivated nor appreciated because it is perceived as not contributing to the cohesiveness of the group. A false consensus forms from believing my ideas are in consensus, end of story.

In my short stint of 18 months as a private in the Army, my first job was to sandpaper the paint off a helmet. As I recall, the sand paper was quite fine and well worn. I was reminded more than once that you don't question[82] why our time was spent sanding. "This is the Army, not a democracy." I was later to learn that you don't question anyone with a rank above you. The need to function as a military unit requires unbending allegiance to authority, something that doesn't come naturally.

Framing and social norms

Here's an example[83] of how Framing can feed group thinking by biasing your judgments towards an acceptable social norm. The effect of using the (back in the day) term Communism in otherwise equivalent questions is notable: ". . . 58 percent of the respondents favored aid to Nicaraguan rebels 'to prevent Communist influence from spreading' [by overthrowing the government], but only 24 percent favored assistance to 'the people [Nicaraguan rebels] trying to overthrow the [Communist] government of Nicaragua.'" The unifying concept of anti-Communism was strong. If you wanted to express dislike of almost anything, you could reasonably hope for agreement by calling it Communist.

---

[82]   He who asks is a fool for five minutes, but he who does not ask remains a fool forever. Chinese proverb.

[83]   Plous68

These studies were done a number of years ago and 'Communism' would today probably be replaced with 'Terrorism'.

The Anchoring and Priming Heuristics

"Two different mechanisms produce anchoring effects—one for each system. There is a form of anchoring that occurs in a deliberate process of adjustment, an operation of System 2. As well, there is anchoring that occurs by a priming effect, an automatic manifestation of System 1."[84] 'Suggestion' is the word used when someone causes us to see, hear, or feel something by merely bringing it to mind. Suggestion is a priming effect, which selectively evokes a compatible response. This response gets absorbed in a quick narrative that serves to find a home for the event within a pattern. Once again we see the perceived importance of making sense of everything, to have it fit in the pattern, to provide some conclusion or closure. It is more comforting (cognitive ease) to have some narrative that, however incorrect, provides us with some context of how to 'understand' what happened.

System 1 understands situations by trying to make them true, and the selective activation of compatible thoughts produces a family of systematic errors that make us gullible and prone to believe too strongly whatever it is we do believe.

Priming is a form of anchoring that works on the level of suggestion. Depending on how a statement is constructed, compatible ideas will be activated. In one study subjects were asked to choose which of two temperatures is closest to the average temperature for a particular local. Subsequently, when words were presented very briefly, those

---

[84]   K2011 pg 120- 122

that chose the higher average temperature more easily identified words associated with the summer time (sun, beach, etc.) while the low temp group more easily identified words associated with winter, like frost and ski.

"Ask someone to pronounce the word spelled by S-H-O-P, then ask them what they do when they come to a green light."[85] This priming sets up the unwary to say . . . 'stop.'

The Anchor Heuristic usually arises from the unintended association of a number (the anchor) with a subsequent predicted value. One study had its subjects write down the last four number of their social security number before being asked to estimate some unknown value like the number of podiatrists in Brooklyn. The results consistently showed that higher predictions could be associated with higher SS#s, the anchors. A similar example of how much irrational power an anchor can have appears when a wheel of fortune with numbers from 1 to 100 is spun. It is rigged to stop on either 10 or 65. Subjects were asked if the number they spun is higher or lower than the percentage of African countries in the United Nations. Subjects then estimated a specific number for the percentage. Results indicated a relation between the magnitude of the spun number and the final estimate of the percentage. Again, a high anchor leads to high estimates.

Why does irrelevant information affect the final estimates? As Lehrer[86] explained it, "In essence, the anchoring effect is about the brain's spectacular inability to dismiss irrelevant information. The problem is that the rational brain isn't good at disregarding facts, even when it knows those facts are useless."

---

[85] Myers pg 26
[86] Lehrer pg 157

Kahneman[87] writes: ". . . an anchoring effect occurs when people consider a particular value for an unknown quantity before estimating that quantity." Anchoring is one of the more curious of the heuristics. "In many situations, people make estimates by starting from an initial value that is adjusted to yield their final answer. The initial value, or starting point, may be suggested by the formulation of the problem, or it may be the result of a partial computation. In either case, adjustments are typically insufficient."[88] System 1 tries to make these numbers coherent with some sensible story.

Here is a study (Piattelli-Palmarini pg 45) of two groups of students that were given 5 seconds to estimate the results of either:

(1) 8 x 7 x 6 x 5 x 4 x 3 x 2 x 1

or

(2) 1 x 2 x 3 x 4 x 5 x 6 x 7 x 8

After five seconds, those students with the sequence starting with 8 x 7 generally had a higher estimate (anchor) of the calculation's true value than the other group. The median results were 2,250 and 512 respectively, the true value is 40,320.

In another experiment the following questions were asked:

"Was Gandhi more or less than 144 years old when he died?

"How old was Gandhi when he died?[89]"

Being exposed to the idea of Gandhi's age at death (144, the anchor) as being somehow related to 144 years

---

[87]   K2011 pg 119
[88]   KT pg 15, 16
[89]   K2011 pg 122

works to give an overly high estimate of how many years he actually lived. S1 tries to make sense of 'Gandhi at 144'. It knows that this is very unlikely so it creates a response with an adjusted age which is typically insufficiently adjusted, but more plausible. "The participants who have been exposed to random or absurd anchors (such as Gandhi's death at age 144) confidently deny that this obviously useless information could have influenced their estimate, and they are wrong."[90]

Anchoring comes into play when selling homes or other goods where it pays to associate the first sell value with a high number. Suppose a pair of shoes sells for $60. One tactic I've seen to promote the sale is to put, on the same price ticket, "Compare at $85." Though this compare comment makes no sense to me otherwise, it is now the reference number, the anchor. The anchoring effect of $85 makes the $60 now seem relatively more of a bargain.

Two groups were asked to estimate the frequency of death from 40 different causes.[91] Group 1 was told that there were about 1,000 deaths per year from electrocution. The other (Group 2) was told there are about 50,000 per year from motor vehicle accidents. The two groups subsequently differed in their frequency estimates of the other 39 causes, Group 1 estimates being significantly lower than Group 2.[92]

A supplier might tilt an audit in his favor by having a nice waiting room with recent technical magazines on display, plus self serving articles and admirable slogans hanging on the wall. Might this first impression bias us just a little before we have even met the receptionist? Might our S1 may be priming us with positive first impressions that lead to subconscious expectations that the supplier will have an operation consistent with those positive primes? We fool

---

[90] K2011 pg 127
[91] K&T pg 481
[92] K&T pg 481

ourselves by supplementing our partial story with coherent, consistent, and confirmatory details. Ambiguity begone!

In an experiment with 2 groups, one saw a brutal beating of a teenager, the other watched something innocuous. The 2 groups then passed judgment on a negligent construction supervisor's actions related to an injury. The first group gave harsher punishment. Sometimes this carryover of an event that primes the subconscious can last longer than we might anticipate and so affects our behavior to a point where we wonder, what were we thinking?[93], [94]

The strength of an anchor can be affected by your physical and mental state. When you are feeling good, you are less likely to make an effort in System 2 adjustments. Feeling good comes from and causes CE (Cognitive Ease). You are in a state of CE when things feel familiar, ambiguity is low, and there is a feeling that you are in the know. On the other hand, when you are hungry, tired, on alert for possible problems, or exhibiting self control, your System 2 is less able to respond to System 1. One kind of exertion, say, controlling our emotions, can deplete your reservoir of effort available to do a physical task.

In a Newsweek article Dec 24, 2012, Oliver Burkeman wrote: ". . . a large (albeit contested) body of evidence suggests that willpower is a unitary and depletable resource: the more of it you use making one change, the less you'll have left over to make others. The discipline you exert on building the exercise habit, at least initially, leaves you more susceptible to burgers rather than less." Living with uncertainty exerts a similar strain on our S2 reserves, so energy has to be spent on resolving ambiguity.

Another factor that can affect the adjustment from an anchor is its precision. "It turns out that a precise anchor

---

[93]   Fine pg 58/9

[94]   K2011 pg 237 ". . . you may feel uneasy in a particular place . . . without having a conscious memory of the triggering event."

is also a stronger anchor—people are less comfortable straying from a precise anchor than a rouned one."[95] You can use rounding to lessen anchoring. There is an implicit uncertainty in rounded numbers. An anchor of the price of a house being $250,000 appears more flexible for a negotiation than a price of $244,300.

Studies indicate that people tend to overestimate the probability of conjunctive events (A and B) and to underestimate the probability of disjunctive events (A or B).[96] These biases are explained as effects of the Anchoring Heuristic. The stated probability of the elementary event (success at any one state) provides a natural starting point for the estimation of the probabilies of both conjunctive and disjunctive events. Since adjustments (calibrations) from the starting point are typically insufficient, the final estimates remain too close to the probabilities of the elementary events in both cases. Note that the overall probability of a conjunctive event (P a+b < P a) is lower that the probability of each elementary event, whereas the overall probability of a disjunctive event (Pa or b > Pa) is higher than the probability of each elementary event. As a consequence of anchoring, the overall probability will be overestimated in conjunctive problems and underestimated in disjunctive problems."[97] See the case of Linda as a further illustration of the conjunctive fallacy at work.

For System 2, the anchor starts the deliberate adjustment process of moving away from the anchor towards an accepted value. A high anchor will lead one group to decrease its estimate, just as a group given a low anchor will adjust upwards. The important conclusion is that the adjustments are insufficient to arrive at an accurate judgment. ". . . a well-intentioned child who turns down

---

[95]   Herbert pg 123
[96]   KT pg 15, 16
[97]   KT pg 15, 16

exceptionally loud music to meet a parent's demand that it be played at a 'reasonable' volume may fail to adjust sufficiently from a high anchor, and may feel that genuine attempts at compromise are being overlooked.[98]"

Trivers pg 65 "You can even manipulate one person's performance in opposite directions by giving opposing primes. Asian women perform better on math tests when primed with "Asian" and worse when primed with "woman".

The Affect heuristic

The Affect heuristic can bias your thinking to achieve a consistency in feelings. For example, a negative feeling about a concept (you name it, like tax increases) leads to inhibition of consideration of possible positive aspects (like better infrastructure) associated with that same concept. If we find the benefits desirable, we will have more trouble finding the risks. This is a result of our excessive need for consistency. We find it difficult to have conflicting feelings for a given concept, a positive feeling about benefits and negative one for risks, so we adjust our feelings to minimize seemingly incompatible differences.

We may like a certain politician's views, and so support him but that feeling can change if one characteristic is found to conflict with what we expected of him. This is why when we detect flip-flopping, we rashly use it to turn our back on all of his politics. We don't like ambiguity, inconsistency, or cognitive dissonance. As seen on Capitol Hill, if you don't like someone, you will be against his proposals, even if they are the same ones you proposed previously. As we used to joke about quality assurance, it's more important to be consistent than to be right.

---

[98]   K2011 pg 121

Framing and the Confirming Bias, the question is the answer.

"The operations of associative memory contribute to a general confirmation bias. When asked, "Is Sam friendly?" different instances of Sam's behavior will come to mind than if you had been asked "Is Sam unfriendly?"[99] In the first case we search our memories for friendly behavior, in the second for unfriendly. This framing process (how the question is asked) can support a deliberate search for confirming evidence that is known as a positive test strategy. Contrary to the philosophical norms of science, which test hypotheses by trying to refute them, people (scientists, quite often) seek data that are likely to be compatible with the beliefs they currently hold. This confirmation bias might apply to a group meeting where the question could be made, 'Is this process reliable?' Here we would expect group members to start looking for information, such as time without an accident that supports an answer of yes, it is reliable. In view of the framing bias, perhaps it's better to ask the question "Is this process unreliable?" especially if we want to challenge a general sense of confidence that the process is reliable. When physicians rephrased "do not resuscitate" as "allow natural death," family members opted for the latter 28% more often.[100]

Bias due to Framing is of particular interest to us because it can lead to violations of the principle of invariance which ". . . asserts that one's choices ought to depend on the situation itself, not on the way it is described. In other words, when we can recognize two descriptions of a situation as equivalent, we ought to make

---

[99] K2011 pg 81.

[100] SA Hidden Metaphors Get under Our Skin: http://www.scientificamerican.com/article/hidden-metaphors-get-under-our-skin/

the same choices for both descriptions."[101] Violations of the invariance principle are sometimes the result of framing effects, because the choice made is dependent on how the situation is presented, or 'framed.'

I found the following to be an interesting example[102] of the kind of biased outcome one can expect from framing.

"Crucial decisions may fall one way or another as a consequence of something as trivial as which way the question has been phrased. People's views about child custody cases, for example, can yield very different outcomes depending on whether they are asked, "Which parent should have custody of the child?" or "Which parent should be denied custody of the child?" In this classic experiment, parent A was moderately well-equipped to have custody in pretty well all respects: income, health, working hours, rapport with the child, and social life. Parent B, by contrast, has a rather more sporadic parental profile. On the one hand, parent B had an above average income and a very close relationship with the child. But on the other, this parent had an extremely active social life, a good deal of work-related travel, and minor health problems. When people were asked who should have custody of the child, they followed the positive test strategy of searching for evidence that each parent would be a good custodian. As a result, parent B's impressive credentials with regard to income and relationship with the child won out over parent A's more modest abilities on these fronts, and nearly two-thirds of participants voted for parent B as the best custodian. Ask

---

[101] Baron pg 264/5
[102] Fine pg 83

who should be denied custody, however, and a very different picture emerged. The positive test strategy yielded evidence of parent's inadequacies as a guardian: the busy social and work life, and the health problems. By comparison, a positive test strategy search of parent A's more pedestrian profile offered no strong reasons for rejection as a guardian. The result: the majority of participants decided to deny parent B custody."

Visual and Cognitive Illusions

A simple way to begin thinking about how heuristics can lead to faulty decisions (cognitive illusions) is to start with some examples of visual illusions.[103]

---

[103] Kahneman Nobel, pg. 465, "the subjective assessment of probability resembles the subjective assessments of physical quantities such as distance or size."

Kahneman, pg 459 Nobel essay, "Perception is reference-dependent: the perceived attributes of a focal stimulus reflect the contrast between the stimulus and a context of prior and concurrent stimuli."

In the following, the two roads are identical, but when placed beside each other, the road on the right always appears more slanted to the right.

The columns below are all the same shade of grey, only the background is changing

The following set of curved blocks are all the same

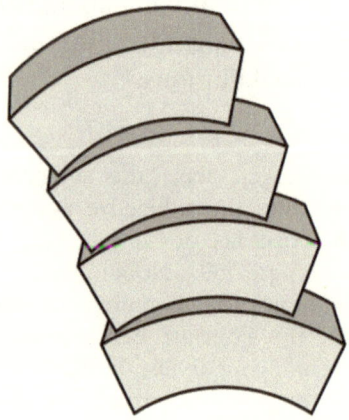

The next two tables are exactly alike

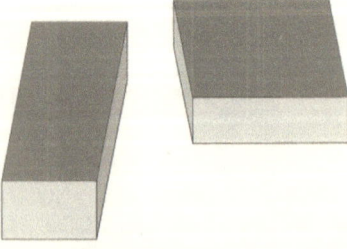

As per Piattelli-Palmarini pg 31, "In the world of perception, an illusion is to reality what a fallacy is to reasoning." Intuitions (S1) share certain characteristics with perceptual illusions in that they occur quickly without conscious thinking, and sometimes are not affected by the rational/analytical thinking system.

I've tried to use these visual illusions as an easy way to illustrate how our heuristic view of the world can sometimes convince us of things that are not true, also known as Cognitive Illusions. As Mark Twain once said, "It ain't what you don't know that gets you into trouble. It's what you know [*your intuition talking*] for sure that just ain't so." And

---

The follwing illusion is quite interesting. The interior of the 'flower' appears bright, yet it has the same reflectance as the page it's printed on. However, this illusion fools us on another level as well. It causes our pupils to constrict, indicating we are reacting to our perceptions, rather than the actual luminance.

Finally, the Müller-Lyer illusion. This is an easy illusion to reproduce, handy as a quick example.

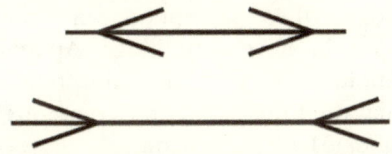

what we know for sure is often a feeling for which we have the least (or least complicated) information.

By way of summary, this chapter introduced experiments that help us understand how a variety of heuristics bias our decisions. Heuristics simplify our decisions in order to resolve them quickly. We make decisions in order to replace the discomfort of ambiguity with confidence of our judgments. We are often gullible enough (we're wired to believe) to accept unjustified patterns[104] or models as representing the truth. There are two major ways of getting it wrong, Type 1 and Type 2. Type 1 (false alarm) seems to have been the predominant error chosen by evolution since it is the most efficient in exploring connections and new models of our world.

The intuitive and rational processes are separated into the S1 and S2 divisions of mind. Emotional (S1) decisions make up much if not most of our decisions. Sometimes S2 gets involved in applying more rational criteria to determine whether to accept or reject the feelings that come from S1. The output of these two systems can change when stress is present. Anchoring, Priming, and Framing, in their various forms, can unconsciously affect our predictions or estimates of probability.

Discrepancies due to intuitive thinking can cause troublesome errors. The sensory system (S1) creates gut feelings which often lead to over-simplification of our judgments. Mostly we thankfully and lazily accept them uncritically. We simplify our decision making by applying the Halo Effect, Group Think, and mimicry to help us reach CE. For better or worse, stereotypes and first

---

[104] In psychology, the perception of connections and meaningfulness in unrelated things. Apophenia can be a normal phenomenon or an abnormal one, as in paranoid schizophrenia when the patient sees ominous patterns where there are none. (MedicineNet.com)

impressions lead us to try to infer the whole from a few of its parts.

Finally we looked at a couple of optical illusions to remind us that just as our visual system sends a message that we are easily fooled, that we can't completely trust our eyes, we need to remember our decisions can also be based on the subconscious part of the mind the workings of which we are not conscious. At least with visual illusions, you know something's wrong.

In the next Chapter we will introduce and go into more depth for the Major Heuristics of Representativeness, Availability, and Affect.

Chapter 3

REPRESENTATIVENESS, AVAILABILITY, AND AFFECT HEURISTICS

Everyman hears only what he understands Goethe

The previous chapter gave an overview of some general information about a variety of heuristics. Here I will add a few examples to further illustrate the Representative, Availability, and Affect Heuristics. This chapter brings attention to the mechanisms that lead to the error of question substitution. Substitution occurs when, if we don't know the answer to a particular question, we answer a different but related one. This results in a Type 3 error which is defined as the right answer to the wrong question.[105]

---

[105] K2011 pg 98 "... when called upon to judge probability, people actually judge something else and believe they have judged probability."

"The advantage of heuristics is that they reduce the time and effort required to make reasonably good judgments and decisions."[106], [107] The disadvantage is that they can be overly simplistic or inappropriate in certain situations. In particular, a problem with heuristics is that other important information such as base rates[108] and data reliability may get neglected, or made subservient to the heuristic. We will focus on these unwanted biases and other errors that heuristics can lead to. This approach of studying the errors of cognitive bias is analogous to a medical researcher's study of disease or trauma in order to understand and promote health.

Risk Analysis often requires some estimates of probability and values (see ICH Q9), calling on us at times to make a best guess for predicted probabilities and interpretation of data patterns. When making these estimates, we need to be aware that our intuitions, our gut feelings, are tied to the unconscious System 1.

Kahneman and Tyverski's 1974 classic "Judgment under uncertainty: Heuristics and biases" concentrated on Representativeness, Availability, and Adjustment and Anchoring as ". . . heuristic principles which reduce the complex tasks of assessing probabilities and predicting values to simpler judgmental operations."[109] Let's start with

---

[106]   Plous pg109

[107]   K2011 pg 151 "Judging probability by representativeness has important virtue: the intuitive impressions that it produces are often—indeed, usually—more accurate than chance guesses would be."

[108]   Base rates are those ratios of occurrences in the population. For example, the occurrence of a characteristic in the population of interest, say 1 in 1,000 (this is the base rate) people have a certain condition.

[109]   K&T pg 6

the representative heuristic[110] to see some examples of how this simplification occurs.

The representative/similarity heuristic

What is the representative heuristic (RH)? From Baron[111] "A person who follows this heuristic evaluates the probability of an uncertain event, or a sample, by the degree to which it is . . . similar in essential properties to its parent population [base rate]; and . . . reflects the salient feature of the process by which it was generated"

Which sequence of heads and tails is more random, i.e., which is more likely to have come from a random process?

H T H H T T H <u>or</u> H H H T T T

The *usual* answer is that the first sequence is more random. We tend to rank sequence 1 as more random than sequence 2 since it appears more likely to have come from a flip of a coin, a random process. It appears more random due to our flawed expectations of the frequency of alteration between heads and tails.[112] Actually, the first

---

[110] K&T pg 163"By this (representativeness) heuristic, an event is judged probable to the extent that it represents the essential features of its parent population or generating process."

[111] Baron pg 150

[112] A distribution of results with an alternation of 50%, (flip a coin, there is a 50% chance that the next flip is the same and 50% that it will be different [alternation]. Studies have shown that short sequences of flips appear more random when the frequency of alternation is set at 70% to 80%. Apparently this happens because at 50%, sequences go longer without altering than we expect from a random number generator. When given the chance to create a random sequence of heads and tails, we tend to avoid long strings of the same heads or tails.

sequence is *less* likely than the second because it is longer. The probability of any sequence of heads and tails is equal to the probability of any other sequence of heads and tails provided that they each have the same number of flips. Making the sequence longer always lowers its probability. The longer a sequence of heads and tails goes without alternating, the less random it appears. This delusion is known as the Gambler's Fallacy, which comes from a misunderstanding of the law of averages, a.k.a. the law of large numbers. After flipping a coin for five heads in a row, consistent with the gambler's fallacy, you bet on a tail, feeling that a tail is overdue, and so deem it more probable than its true 50/50 chance. Fooled by a feeling. We forget that the coin forgets, it has no memory. It's always a 50/50 chance of heads or tails[113], a 50% chance of alternating or staying the same on each flip.

The bias caused by the RH is that in this case the wrong choices are made in a consistent way (and so referred to as systemic error, or equivalently, bias), leading to the first sequence being incorrectly chosen. For some, this delusion is on par with an optical illusion[114] in that no matter how we try to counteract it, it still fools us. Almost as difficult is changing your beliefs to accept the truth that a sequence of heads, heads, tails, heads, tails (HHTHT) is obtained with the same probability as all five tosses being heads (HHHHH). We intuitively feel we know what randomness is, and five heads in a row isn't it. It's easier to

---

[113] What are the chances that when flipping a coin, you predict the correct heads or tails fourteen times in a row? That's what happened when the NFC won the coin toss at the 2011 Super Bowl. That tale of the toss, not necessarily a toss of a tail, marked the 14th consecutive year that the NFC had correctly called the flip.

[114] Cognitive illusions differ from optical illusions in that "They are somewhat embarrassing and they appear avoidable." K&T pg 493

imagine an illusory pattern (and so non-random) in this second sequence and explanatory patterns are comforting. Randomness on the other hand is patternless by definition. You would have to work harder to create a pattern in the first sequence, so it is perceived to be more likely from a random process. Who wants to do that? You stick with your gut feeling, your first impression, your evaluation of probability via representativeness.

When pressed for time or resources, we tend to ease those decisions concerning complex events by using simpler scenarios. What starts as the question of what is more likely, morphs into what is the simpler scenario of what is more imaginable. If the question is too hard, change the question.[115]

The Tom W. experiment

One group of subjects was asked to estimate the proportion of graduate students in nine different fields of graduate study. Their answers constituted the base rates for the following two parts of the experiment.

A second group was given a description of a fictitious character named Tom[116] as being stereotypically smart but nerdy, not very social, etc. They were then asked how similar Tom was to students in each of the nine programs. Not

---

[115] K&T pg 177 "Many of the events whose likelihood people wish to evaluate depend on several interrelated factors. Yet it is exceedingly difficult for the human mind to apprehend sequences of variations of several interacting factors. We suggest that in evaluating the probability of complex events only the simplest and most available scenarios are likely to be considered."

[116] K2011 pg 148 "Tom W was intentionally designed as an 'anti-base-rate' character, a good fit to small fields [of study] and a poor fit for the most populated specialties."

surprisingly, he was determined to be least similar to social science students, and most like those in computer science.

A third group of students was presented with Tom's description, but in addition were told that it had been written years ago and was not considered reliable. This group was asked the probability that Tom was a student in each of the nine graduate fields. Their answers gave the same ranking as the second group, but had no relation to the baseline[117] that the first group provided. Simply put, the evaluations of the probability of Tom's field of study were substituted by the evaluation of Tom's similarity (representativeness) to students in those programs. The question about probability was difficult but the substituted question about similarity was easier so it was answered instead.[118] Substitution was perfect in this case: there was no indication that the participants did anything else but judge representativeness. Information that doesn't matter, such as an unreliable description of Tom, shouldn't matter, but it did. It's hard to ignore new information, even in a case like this where it was clear that the information labeled 'unreliable' should have been disregarded. "You surely understand in principle that worthless information should not be treated differently from a complete lack of information. WYSIATI [What You See Is All There Is] makes it very difficult to apply that principle."[119] Information you have just been exposed to doesn't disappear just because

---

[117] Baron pg 147. Groups 2 and 3 were unaware of the base rate prepared by group 1. It was assumed that had groups 2 and 3 prepared the base rate, their results would have been similar to those of group 1. For group 3, given that they knew nothing (invalid characterization) about Tom, some thought should have been given as to the probability of a random student being enrolled in being in any of the graduate programs, essentially some consideration of the base rate.

[118] K2011 pg 148-9

[119] K2011 pg 153

you have been told it is irrelevant. A judge instructs a jury to disregard a comment, but studies show that it falls on deaf ears. It is of interest that base rate information was ignored, while unreliable descriptive information was used to answer the question even though it had been discredited. This is another case of us being more comfortable with a story, than a statistical review. With no information on Tom, the best guess of his probability of being in any particular program should have come from the first group's baseline which included relative number of graduate students in various fields. In this regard a common theme in this book is that our brains are wired to appreciate and accept narrative information while it is with greater difficulty that we consider, if at all, generalized information such as averages and percentages.

Base rate and data reliability neglect in the Doctor / Lawyer choice

In another example,[120] "Subjects were shown brief personality descriptions of several individuals, allegedly sampled at random from a group of 100 professionals— engineers and lawyers. The subjects were asked to assess, for each description, the probability that it belonged to an engineer rather than to a lawyer." Regardless of whether the subjects were told that the percentages (base rates) were 70% lawyer and 30% engineer, or vice versa, they gave the same probability, 50%. Representativeness trumped base rates. When subjects were not given any descriptive information, they made use of the base rate. When a job neutral (uninformative) description was given, base rates

---

[120]   K&T pg 5

again were ignored and results tended to 50% lawyer / 50% engineer.[121]

The RH is responsible for the diversion of attention away from the reliability of the information. When we find a pattern in our data, we focus on that to the exclusion of the quality of the information and the context (base rate). In risk analysis, there are opportunities to rely on intuition to produce probability estimates. Caution is advised, because gut feelings may be based on outdated or otherwise irrelevant experience. Even if the data is numerical and relevant, care must be taken to assure that the measurement system is adequate. We often treat our measurements as if they do not vary, either in time (stability) or in response to different operators and other variables (ruggedness). When we view a result with this blind faith, we will act as if that all variation comes from our product, and none from the instruments and people that measure it. This can lead to ineffective corrective and preventive actions.

The RH is often the reason why we give biased answers when asked to determine the probability that an event or behavior came from a particular population or process. An example:

Consider the following experiment of how representativeness interferes with our sense of statistical intuition. Participants were told that a large number of samples of six children were taken from a population where the number of boys (B) and girls (G) is equal. The sequence GBGGBG was found 72 times.

They are then asked, for this same population, how many times do you estimate the sequence BGBBBB occurred? What happens when an immediate solution does not come to mind? The RH rephrases the original question with how

---

[121] K&T pg 5 "Evidently, people respond differently when given no evidence and when given worthless evidence."

much does the event appear to be like the population of 50/50 boys/girls. The median estimate of what the frequency would be in the same large sample was 30.

The reason for this error (the two sequences are equally likely, and so should be estimated to occur at the same frequency) is that the first sequence appears (but isn't) more random, and therefore judged more likely to have come from and be representative of a random process. This problem invokes the heuristic of representativeness or similarity. The 'rule' here is if the sample appears similar to or typical of the parent population, it is judged more likely. This example also triggered the tongue in cheek 'law of small numbers'[122] attributed to Kahneman and Tverski. This 'law' being as Kahneman (pg 36) wrote: "The law of large numbers assures that the very large samples are highly representative of the populations from which they are drawn . . . we have characterized the expectancy of local representativeness as a belief in the law of small numbers, according to which "the law of large numbers applies to small numbers as well." In other words, we expect small samples to be representative of the large population it came from. This expectation is unfounded in reality, but is not excluded in our heuristical rules of thumb.[123] The first sequence appears to better match our sense of randomness, so we estimate that it will be a more common (more representative of the population it came from) result than the less random appearing second sequence.

"One feature of the RH is an excessive willingness to predict the occurrence of unlikely (low base-rate) events. Here is an example. You see a person reading The New York Times on the New York subway. Which of the following

---

[122] Also known as the homogeneity bias.
[123] Short sequences are biased because they cannot accommodate the long runs that can occur in a random process. You can't see that a run of 4 in a sample of 4 is part of a run of 7.

is a better bet to be the reading stranger? She has a PhD. or she does not have a college degree."[124] While on one level the PhD option seems a reasonable and representative choice, there are more non degree travelers than PhDs on the train and that base rate needs to be kept in mind. We need to know how many people are on the train and how many of them are PhDs and how many don't have a degree. For the RH, because the consideration of a base rate is generally close to imperceptible, it is often left out of the evaluation. The reason for this base rate neglect, as the chapter on stories will reinforce, is that generally we are influenced more by anecdotes and narratives (the imagined visual of a woman reading the Times) than more abstract concepts like base rates, probabilities,[125] and averages.

The above examples illustrate why we have problems correctly answering risk analysis problems such as ranking by probability with 'which is the most likely?' kind of questions. We may be answering a different question from that which was asked. Tough (probability) questions are replaced with easier (judgmental) ones. Asked which sequence is more random gets substituted by which one *appears* more random, and appearances can be deceiving. Simplification by question substitution due to the RH often begs for further analysis. Due diligence of data quality is, well, due.

Risk and Randomness in Pattern Detection

Randomness is truly too important to be left to chance, or our statistical intuition of it.

In this section risk management is what we do every time we make a decision made with incomplete

---

[124] K2011 pg 151
[125] Gigerenzer Rationality, pg 150 "The term *probabilitas* originally referred to an opinion backed by authority."

information. If we knew that it would rain tomorrow, there really wouldn't be an internal debate as to whether to bring an umbrella. Predictability being imperfect due to the unknown factors, we can informally assess the risks and benefits of a sampling of choices and decide what's best. We leave the ice scraper in the car in the winter because there is no cost to doing so. We keep a spare in the car always, because the additional cost of transporting its extra weight is imperceptible, and while the need for doing so should be very infrequent, the regret for not doing so is something we surely want to avoid.

How does misunderstanding of randomness relate to risk analysis? The case presented above (HHTHT vs HHHHH) showed that because we can find patterns where randomness (by definition without pattern) reigns, we may willingly go on a wild goose chase searching for a special (non-random) cause to explain our results. Put the two sequences on a control or run chart and the conclusion will still be that there's nothing special about the first sequence, while the second one begs for an explanation. Patterns, even the ones that only exist in our imaginations, feed the need to predict and explain results because they appear to contain signals instead of the noise they are.

The following[126] takes this application of patterns to randomness to the extremes, to what we might call superstition[127]. Pigeons were fed at random intervals and then feeding stopped. When the pigeon got hungry it repeated whatever it was doing the last time it was fed, as if hoping its hopping had some effect in getting food. The Trobriand Islander cargo cults located in the South Pacific, thought that by building life size models of the planes that once were associated with better conditions, they could

---

[126] Shermer pg 77
[127] A superstition is a premature explanation that overstays its time. George Iles

lure back the real airplanes and the cargo they carried. If an airplane-like object sat on their runway they believed the associated cargo would follow. Similarly, we're not above being superstitious in our attempts to pair good or bad luck with some behavioral pattern we can control. Sports and gambling have a rich history of players and fans continuing to do what they were doing when a win happened. The superstitious mind converts a spurious association into a causal relationship. We like to fool ourselves into thinking that we have control, and so too easily we determine correlations to be causations in our cognitive illusions.

Risk management is ideally based on a solid knowledge of the process. It's difficult to accept that randomness, which we cannot predict and are not in control of, is the explanatory agent for some behavior of the process. Misunderstanding of how random effects and natural variation makes us struggle with the concept that just because one number is not the same as another, that is not enough to assure they are different. The difference may be explained by randomness. Just because four values in a row are above average does not mean there has been a shift in the process. Just because five values in a row are decreasing, does not mean there is a trend. Just because a statistical test does not indicate a significant difference between two groups does not mean that they are the same. It could be randomness of the process and imprecision of the measurement. Check your sample and effect size, find the variance, and calculate the power (capability) to detect a real difference. Understand what's critical to the quality of your measurements and estimates. Since we are generally not satisfied with the explanation that the cause of an apparent pattern is due to randomness (hey, shtuff happens), we search for a reason (plane present, random movements occurring before feeding) to assign some palpable cause for the association. We feel uncomfortable with the abstract, uncontrollable factor that is randomness.

It's much more satisfying if we can find a cause that is easily imagined or visualized. We are quick to identify causes of effects, nonexistent though they may be. This bias to expect and find a pattern may be justified as an evolutionary advantage, as we shall see later.

Another way that risk analysis can be biased occurs when processes are in control. For example, by using a control or run chart to detect and respond to apparent trends, we may feel (S1) that we have detected an upward trend in some variable. If this apparent trend is just another misunderstanding of the effects of randomness, our adjustments to the process will be over adjustments, and tampering, and control will slip away.

As an example in the risk analysis world, management may want a quick turnaround on the question of what the probability is that some unusual sequence of data points comes from a possible trend in the process. You don't have time to determine if a true trend is occurring or if it is just a common chance event. You look at the data and remember a few times something similar occurred. On those occasions the data returned to expected in control behavior without any intervention, and the product was not found to be compromised. You give your educated, but subjective determination that the current, somewhat unusual data is similar to a few situations in the past when they could be said to have not been part of a trend, just randomness at play. Maybe you're right and maybe you're wrong, either way, you didn't answer the question, how likely is it that this data is trending, that it is out of control? You answered the question of how alike the data was to previous data. Your gut said go forward with the production, go forward with the cold launch. Blame it on the RH.

Our focus on representativeness also takes attention away from the evaluation of the reliability[128] of the

---

[128]   K2011 pg 153 "insensitivity to the quality of evidence."

information. "This is a serious mistake, because judgments of similarity and probability are not constrained by the same logical rules. It is entirely acceptable of judgments of similarity to be unaffected by base rates and also by the possibility that the description was inaccurate, but anyone who ignores base rates and the quality of evidence in probability assessments will certainly make mistakes."[129] Since S1 doesn't filter its own signals, it will pay only enough attention to the quality of its information to assure it is plausible, not necessarily the best. Combine this WYSIATI MO with a non-responding S2 and if S2 is unable to filter S1, then probabilities of representativeness shall surely be compromised and biased.

Kahneman suggests relying even more on base rates when reliability of the description is uncertain. In particular, when our memories are relied on for decisions, information quality again becomes an issue.

Information reliability can be an important factor in risk analysis. Historical data used to support risk analysis often comes in the form of a Pareto chart. Pareto charts are fine if the process is stable. The analysis then broadens to require an observation of behavior over time, in other words, control or run charts. This combination of analytical tools becomes much more valuable when used together to determine where resources would be best used, one of the deliverables we should expect from risk analysis. Pareto charts can be used to establish base rates, and for this, robust frequencies are required to assure the process is in control. A high frequency cause on a Pareto chart is attractive as a potential area to invest resources. However, a run or control chart may reveal the recent process to be free of this cause, and so it may no longer be a good starting place to improve the process.

---

[129] K2011 pg 149/50

Feelings precede conscious analysis. You already 'know' how you feel about taking the chance before you put it under the scrutiny of System 2. System 1 quickly puts what it finds into a plausible scenario, and our sense of cognitive ease adjusts to how cohesive that narrative is. A good story makes us comfortable and so our guard (System 2) gets let down. Herbert narrates[130] a story of three experienced skiers and the decision they took that lead to their death. 'Twas the season for avalanches' and the pass they attempted was no stranger to such events. What were they thinking? Perhaps it went something like, "It's a nice day, I've never been in an avalanche anywhere, much less here, and we're in the company of experts who have thought out a prudent route. Let's go." This story doesn't make us anxious, just the opposite. It puts us into a familiar story, a familiar pattern, one we recognize, one that hasn't been tainted with the worry of risks. We are optimistic when it comes to risks.[131] Bad things happen to other people, not us. We imagine what a good run we are going to have, just like we have had so many times before. If these skiers had been novices, perhaps there would have been more discussion, less trust in the experts and history. One problem with establishing a past is that we tend to cherry pick the information that agrees with our feelings. Over time this leads to creeping determinism as we reconstruct our memories in favor of our current beliefs. We misremember conflicting information. This serves to strengthen the confirmation bias that leads to an irrational

---

[130] From the Introduction to his book

[131] Blackpg141 "To take an obvious example, think about how many people divorce. Almost all of them are acquainted with the statistic that between one-third and one-half of all marriages fail, something the parties involved did not forecast while trying the knot. Of course, 'not us,' because 'we get along so well' (as if others tying the knot got along poorly.)"

perseverance in continuing on ahead. It's hard to admit you made a mistake and even more difficult to turn back.

K2011 pg 80 **A BIAS TO BELIEVE AND CONFIRM.** Believing is a product of System 1, skepticism as an attribute of System 2. If System 2 is occupied ('keep these numbers in your memory while we test you"), you will be more gullible, more likely to believe anything since System 2 is not available to judge System 1. System 1 believes, and tries to convince System 2 to follow. A rested S2 will assume nothing important is going on, as compared to System 1, that thinks that something is always going on, though generally it's not of much interest.

As a common example of substituting a question due to lack of representativeness, "We rely on representativeness when we judge the potential leadership of a candidate for office by the shape of his chin or the forcefulness of his speeches."[132] More recent investigations indicate politicians with 'baby faces' are thought of as being more trustworthy. Either way, the unconscious works with what it has, and makes a quick evaluation of leadership based on appearance which shouldn't matter.

Availability Heuristic

"Get your facts first, then you can distort them as much as you please." Mark Twain

What is availability? "According to Amos Tversky and Daniel Kahneman (1974, pg 1127), the availability heuristic is a rule of thumb by which decision makers ". . . assess the frequency of a class or the probability of an event by the ease with which instances or occurrences can be brought to mind." Usually this heuristic works quite well; all things

---

[132] K2011 pg 157

being equal, common events are easier to remember or imagine than are uncommon events. By relying on availability to estimate frequency and probability, decision makers are able to simplify what might otherwise be very difficult judgments.[133]

For example, subjects listened to a list of people's names and were then asked which sex was more frequent in the list. Subjects tended to erroneously choose the sex that included the higher percentage of *famous* males or females, not the higher percentage of total males or females. The famous were more available, more salient, and so judged more frequent. Here System 1 changes the original (how frequent) question to a simpler one (how salient).[134]

Availability is affected by how easily an event is recalled or how easily many instances of it are recalled. It can also be affected by the ease with which the event can be constructed, or even the perceived ease of imagining how difficult it would be to construct. If a single recent event is very salient, emotionally engaging, or has been experienced directly, availability may be expected to be consistent with a higher estimate of probability than the true frequency. The estimated probability of a plane crash goes up after one has occurred. Insurance companies feed on this perception, this exaggerated fear.

While the Availability Heuristic is a reasonable rule, ". . . there are cases in which the general rule of thumb breaks down and leads to systematic biases. Some events are more available than others not because they tend to occur frequently or with high probability, but because they are inherently easier to think about."[135] Recollection of memories can be eased if stereotyping was associated with the event to be recalled.

---

[133] Plous pg 121.
[134] K2011 pg 131
[135] Plous pg 121

I think the availability heuristic holds a special place[136] as a cause of bias because there are so many ways to see its influence in decision making. Let's look at some examples.

Consider the experiment[137] where spouses were asked for their per cent contribution to chores in the house, i.e., how much taking out the trash, washing dishes, sweeping the floor, etc. that they did compared to their spouse. Logically, the total percent of a chore should be 100%, but as expected, each individual more easily remembered their own contributions as evidenced by the combined estimated contributions being above 100%. This difference in availability (my memories of my contributions are more available than my memories of her contributions) lead to the inaccuracy of the estimate for frequencies, and this inaccuracy is biased to make me look good.

This egocentric bias associated with who is doing the most chores can be extended to include your own contributions as being more available when working in a group. You will be biased to recall and hence believe your contributions are more frequent than other members. Or you might find your group's contributions greater than other groups.

If everybody is subject to this bias, then like in Lake Wobegon, you'll find ". . . the children are all above average." Mirror, mirror, on the wall, who's the fairest of them all? The answer we all expect is 'you are, of course'. Overestimating the goodness of your family, your friends, or yourself are all driven by the availability heuristic to create a myside bias. You *are* a better than average driver, right?

Which is more likely, a word that starts in English with a K, or has K as the third letter? You try to think of examples of each (this is the availability heuristic), and you find it is

---

[136] K2011 pg 142 ". . . . all heuristics are equal but availability is more equal than the others."

[137] K2011 pg 131

easier to think of words that start with K. Because you find it easier to think of words that start with K, you decide K's are more frequent, which is wrong. Baron pg 153.

In the following example we have an example of Availability leading to the Conjunctive Fallacy. This bias is also covered in chapter four, Why We Don't Change. Subjects were asked which is more common, seven letter words that end with 'ing' or seven letter words where the 6th letter was 'n'. Again we try to find examples and again we find that it is easier to imagine a word that is not the most frequent word. In this case, seven letter words with the sixth letter 'n' are a subset of seven letter words ending in 'ing', so they can't be more frequent, that would be the Conjunction Fallacy.

Vividness can increase the availability and so the estimate of probability. If you hear of the crash of an airplane with a famous person or group on board, you are likely to overestimate the probability of it happening to you. The more detail, the more memorable. We remember the occurrence of individuals killed and maimed, not the non-occurrence. The media helps by reporting the hits, not the misses, not the silent evidence.

How information is presented also has an effect on how vividly, and so memorable, we perceive an event. Vividness is supported by detail, so that we expect a vivid memory of an event and its details should make the event appear more probable. But as we will see in the Linda experiment, adding details also lowers the probability of an event at the same time that it is making it easier to bring an event to memory.

Which is more likely?

1. A massive fire which began in Oklahoma is still burning in this hot, dry summer.
2. A massive fire is still burning in this hot, dry summer.

The inclusion of "which began in Oklahoma" makes the first statement easier to visualize, making the first statement more available and so judged more likely. On the other hand, the extra detail sets up another instance of the conjunction fallacy so that it is actually less likely.

"When it comes to probability and frequency estimates, no heuristic is more central than the availability heuristic."[138] (See also Gigerenzer Simple . . . pg 213-214.) "At this point, the operation of availability is 'one of the most widely shared assumptions in decision making, as well as in social judgment research.'"

The reliance on the availability of memory is central, and so anything that affects the accuracy of memories affects our probability estimates.

Availability is sometimes confused with the representativeness heuristic. This confounding can appear when a question of probability or ranking evokes both a readily available and representative response.

The Linda experiment

The following is an old but instructive example of undue emphasis on availability.

The description of a fictitious woman indicates "Linda is 31 years old, single, outspoken and very bright. She majored in philosophy. As a student she was deeply concerned with issues of discrimination and social justice and also participated in antinuclear demonstrations."

---

[138] Plous 130

A number of additional descriptions of Linda were listed for the respondent to rank the likelihood of being correct. The descriptions were:

1. Is a teacher in an elementary school
2. Works in a book store and takes yoga classes
3.   Is active in the feminist movement
4. Is a psychiatric social worker
5. Is a member of the League of Woman Voters
6. Is a bank teller
7. Is an insurance salesperson
8. Is a bank teller and active in the feminist movement.

Please rank each description from 1 to 8 (please don't skip to the results) in order of decreasing likelihood.

In this experiment, #3 was rated as highly likely, #6 as low, but #8 as more likely than #6. This can't be true.[139] There must be a higher number of total bank tellers than bank tellers who are also active in the feminist movement. This is like saying red balloons are more common than balloons. This error is called the Conjunction Fallacy[140] and

---

[139] Plous (T&K) pg 111, "As the amount of detail in a scenario increases, its probability can only decrease steadily but its representativeness and hence its apparent likelihood may increase." Similarly, added detail increases belief in representativeness as higher precision increases anchoring power. Plous pg 112 ". . . specific scenarios appear more likely than general does ones because they are more representative of how we imagine particular events."

[140] Gigerenzer Mortals pg 12 argues the conjunction fallacy depends on the meaning we give the word 'and'. If "librarian and feminist" was interpreted as being separate groups (10 librarians and 5 feminists) the likelihood that Linda was a member of both would be greater than if she was a member of the group that was the intersection of the two groups, librarians and feminists. For example, if we were new to the neighborhood and we say we invited friends and neighbors to a cook out,

it occurs here because the availability heuristic overpowers other considerations. The image of Linda as active in the feminist movement seems more easily imagined but less likely, if she also has a job.

In the practice of risk analysis, this kind of error could have an influence on the subjective determination of which cause, among various, could be the most likely to produce a failure. If the question of availability replaces the actual question of likelihood, wrong answers await. Here again is an example of inappropriate simplification made by substituting a probability prediction (i.e., Which description is more likely?) with an easier, subconscious question of 'Which description is more available?'

Inversion confusion

The availability heuristic incorrectly inverts the rule of "because it is frequent, I remember" to "because I remember, it must be frequent". That these two are not necessarily equivalent is witnessed by Alice in Wonderland,[141] the O.J. Simpson case, or by the probability inversion calculated in Appendix 6.

---

we are not talking about just friends who are neighbors, we mean both friends and neighbors, mostly separate groups, even though a few could be both. That is, if we just invited friends, these would be different individuals from just inviting neighbors. This is contrasted with the interpretation leading to the conjunction fallacy that both characteristics reside in the same person.

[141] "Then you should say what you mean," the March Hare went on. "I do" Alice hastily replied; "at least—at least I mean what I say—that's the same thing, you know." "Not the same thing a bit!" said the Hatter. "Why, you might just as well say that 'I see what I eat' is the same thing as 'I eat what I see'!" (a seefood diet?)

For instance, the probability that a Spanish citizen speaks Spanish is not the same as its inversion, the probability that if one speaks Spanish, he is a Spanish citizen.

From the O.J. Simpson trial where he was accused of killing his wife, the defense argued that because there is a low probability (about 1/1000) of a beater later killing the woman, the fact that Simpson beat his wife is not relevant. Actually it is this line of reasoning that is not relevant. Because she was battered doesn't mean that the batterer would murder her, but because she was murdered, most likely a boyfriend/husband who had previously battered her did it. If a man abuses his wife and she is later murdered, the husband is the murderer a relatively high percent of the time.

Salience, Vividness, and frequency estimations

For availability to be a reliable measure of frequency, it should *only* be influenced by frequency, but unfortunately, it is also influenced by other factors.[142] When asked for probabilities or frequencies, the question is substituted by salience (Congressmen, movie stars, athletes), vividness (media reports of flooding, plane crashes, thievery), and personal experience (it happened to me). All of these variables can affect the availability of an answer when we are questioned to estimate probabilities and frequencies.[143]

---

[142]   K&T pg 11: "Availability is a useful clue for assessing frequency or probability, because instances of large classes are usually reached better and faster than instances of less frequent classes. However, availability is affected by factors other than frequency and probability. Consequently, the reliance on availability leads to predictable biases"

[143]   K2011 pg 130

The case of the wrong choice in the previously discussed case of Linda the bank teller is also due in part to the availability heuristic. It is somehow easier for us to imagine (more easily brought to mind) that Linda is a feminist bank teller than to imagine her as just a bank teller. While the availability heuristic might normally be a good probability predictor, this example shows us how it can also lead to illogical and wrong decisions. In risk analysis we might be biased toward overweighting recently found root causes[144] just because they are more mentally available. In Linda's case a more detailed description makes the choice less probable, yet unfortunately, more frequently chosen due to easier mental recall or construction.

Emotions and decisions, the Affect Heuristic

When stressed for time (System 2 can't keep up) or resources (see K2011 pg 44 for hunger), we tend to ease those decisions concerning complex events by using simpler scenarios. What starts as the question of what is more likely, morphs into what is the simpler scenario of what is more based on feelings. If the question is too hard, change the question.

Overweighting of the fear factor is another type of error related to accessibility. Since we tend to think of anecdotes that are more easily imagined than non-events, we easily bring to mind and tend to overestimate the probability of events related to fearful conditions. Nevertheless, while fears have the power to bias decisions, there is some level of fear that is "healthy". As mentioned earlier, the extreme

---

[144] This recency effect could extend to a recently attended seminar/webinar where a certain corrective action tool was emphasized. When all you remember is the seminar tool, a hammer, all problems start to look like nails.

state of fearlessness can get you into trouble. Sometimes the bear *is* in the bush. This also can be applied to risk management in that recent past problems may loom larger (have a heavier weighting) than they deserve. We fear they will occur again, so we over react, so we won't get fooled again, so we won't regret our decision. Risk management should help us assign appropriate resources to problems based on scientific analysis. Here we want to make sure we get the best probabilities, not necessarily the easiest availability.

K2011 pg 144 How would you feel about allowing your teen-age daughter to go to a rock/rap concert for the first time? "You may know that there is really (almost) nothing to worry about, but you cannot help images and anecdotes of bad things from coming to mind. As Slovic has argued, the amount of concern is not adequately sensitive to the probability of harm; you are imagining the numerator—the tragic story you saw on the news—and neglect the denominator (the non-events). Sunstein has coined the phrase "probability neglect" and Slovic called it "denominator neglect" to describe this overemphasis on occurrences by neglecting non-occurrences.

As an example of the overweighting effect of vividness on decision making, student participants were asked which of two urns they thought was the best bet to draw a winning marble out of. Winning marbles are red. In a small urn, one of the ten marbles was red. In a larger urn, eight out of one hundred marbles was red. Surprisingly, about one in three participants chose the larger, less likely to win urn. The clear image of eight vibrant red marbles was often sufficient to choose the urn less likely to win. In a similar experiment, subjects were asked which has greater risk; 1,286 out of 10,000 or 24.4 out of 100. You know it, the former was judged more dangerous than the latter. Kahneman[145] gives

---

[145]   K2011 pg 329

another example. A vaccine has a 0.001% chance of causing permanently disability. Looked at another way, 1 in 100,000 children will be permanently disabled. The vivid element 'children' is enough to make this second description appear a greater risk than the first description.

There are always going to be risks as long as we cannot perfectly predict the future. The existence of risks implies that we don't have all the information needed to be sure of our decisions. Our job is to get the most bang (reduced risk) for our buck in resource allocation. These examples should be informative as to why the base rate (mostly uninteresting non-events) is often neglected. Without the base (the denominator, the number of possibilities, what happened plus what didn't) there is no base rate. The WYSIATI System 1 does not operate in terms of averages and probabilities and base rates. That is the job of System 2. System 1 constructs anecdotes, and from these, convincing emotions. It dwells in the story telling mode, and the more cohesive the story, the more convincing it is. The aim of its stories (to be covered in greater detail in Chapter 5) is sufficient plausibility, not best probability. There is no time for S1 to judge what's best, just what's adequate.

"The Affect (regret, emotion) Heuristic is another opportunity for substitution, in which the answer to an easy question (How do I feel about it?) serves as an answer to the much harder original question (What do I think about it?)." "Consistent affect is a central element of what I have called associative coherence."[146] It's harder to find benefits in something you find risky (not coherent) or that you don't like. Coherence (it's ALL good) increases the perception, the probability of the story being true.

". . . imagining an outcome does not guarantee that it will appear more likely; if an outcome is difficult to envision, the attempt to imagine it may actually reduce the

---

[146]   K2011 pg 139

perceived likelihood that it will occur."[147] In this respect, when asked to list instances of an event or situation, initial instances may come to mind easily, but as time wore on it becomes more difficult to continue. The feeling you are left with (because it became harder to continue imagining it) is that its availability is low even though you were able to list several instances of it happening.

If there is frequent worry about a subject, the availability may be high because it is on the mind frequently. Because it is thought about frequently and so easily available, it is judged to occur frequently. On the other hand, if the thought process is difficult because of the emotional nature of the event, or because we are trying hard to come up with additional instances of the event, then in these cases the increased amount of thinking about the subject, because it is difficult, can result in a lower estimate of the probability of the event.[148]

Percentage Wise (not) and Natural Frequency (counts)

Natural frequencies (Gigerenzer) are more vivid than percentages, and so tend to be overweighted. "In one experiment[149], professionals evaluated whether it was safe to discharge from the psychiatric hospital a patient, Mr. Jones, with a history of violence. The information they received included an expert's assessment of the risk. The same statistics were described in two ways:

(A) Of every 100 patients similar to Mr. Jones, 10 are estimated to commit an act of violence against

147   Plous pg 125
148   Plous pg 125
149   K2011 pg 330

others during the first several months after discharge.

(B) Patients similar to Mr. Jones are estimated to have a 10% probability of committing as act of violence against others during the first several months after discharge.

The professionals who saw the frequency format (A) were almost twice as likely to deny the discharge, (41%, compared to 21% in the probability format (B). The more vivid (people vs. percentages) presentation produces a higher decision weight for the same probability." Not good. This same lesson that we respond better to natural frequencies than probabilities occurred in an episode of the television show 'House' where a patient was told she had an 80% chance of survival. Her immediate and frightened response was "So you mean I have a one chance in five of dying?" She was thinking in the concrete, in her personal probability of dying, while the doctor was thinking in abstract averages.

What's available? Stuff that's salient. What's salient? Stuff that stands out as not fitting our usual thoughts on how things are. Surprises. In a world mostly not disturbing, we find news of a robbery in our neighborhood or of a famous personality getting into trouble to be salient.

When asked for leading causes of death, accidents were rated more frequent than disease, though the opposite was true. Accidents are more salient. News media dramatize and reinforce the salience of certain types of events. How often do they report a plane flight without incident?

The ICH Q9 Quality Risk Management document, used in the pharmaceutical industry as guidance for understanding and controlling quality (as opposed to financial) risk, presents a scientific approach to making decisions. ISO 14971 defines "risk" as "combination of the probability of occurrence of harm and the severity of harm". The determination of these probabilities may not be as entirely objective as anticipated.

While researching some of the technical aspects that apply to risk management a couple of years ago, I came across a reference that piqued my curiosity. What place would a book titled "The Psychology of Judgment and Decision Making" have in the literature of scientific risk analysis and management? I guess my surprise came from my underlying assumption that when we all have the same information, assuming our decisions are rational and scientific, individual judgments should be very similar. Not only did I think we should share the same decisions between experts, but also within experts: all other things being equal, our decisions should consistently be the same today as they were yesterday. What was I thinking?

Understanding that variation permeates everything we do, I could also understand that sometimes the result of any process is sometimes a little more, sometimes a little less, but since this kind of random error, sometimes referred to as systematic error, is usually small, it shouldn't be much of a problem. Biased accuracy based on our subconscious minds is another matter. At the very least, I wouldn't expect that our decisions could be swayed by how we are feeling at the moment, how the question was asked, or how good logic could be overrun by our subconscious.

The FDA wants the pharmaceutical industry to use good science to understand and manage the risks in their products and processes. To that end they have suggested several basic statistical tools in the ICH Q9 document on Risk Management. When there is insufficient data to apply these tools effectively (imagine a histogram with only five data points), and additional data is either too costly or impossible to obtain, there aren't many options but to estimate the probability of risk subjectively. I have found the ISPE Volume 7 Risk-Based Manufacture of Pharmaceutical Products First Edition / September 2010 A Guide to

Managing Risks Associated with Cross-Contamination to be usefull. In reference to this document, note that on page 9 there is a reference to risk aversion ("Regulators also may adopt risk adverse strategies, particularly during inspections.") Also 6.2.1 refers to qualitative risk analysis, the results of which may indicate the need for a quantitative analysis. "The output of risk evaluation is either a quantitative estimate (e.g. a numerical probability) or a qualitative description (e.g. high, medium, low) of a range of risk." Unfortunately, subjective estimates of both qualitative and quantitative data can be biased.[150] In

---

[150] Making any kind of measurement or numerical estimate results in values that can be characterized by their accuracy (bias) and precision (variability). Our concern here will be accuracy since heuristics have the potential to create bias. Accuracy is basically the difference between the true value and the measured or estimated value. When we refer to a value as being highly accurate, the result of this accuracy calculation is a relatively small value. If the measurements are either (1) consistently above or (2) consistently below the true value, the measurement is considered to be biased (also referred to as systematic error).

Random vs Systemic error. Proofiness pg 103 I quote the following about polling practices as an example of how we can mistake/miss probabilities due to systematic (biased) error while controlling for random errors. "The margin of error only represents statistical error, the inaccuracy inherent to using a sample of a population to try to represent the world. While that error is extremely important—it cannot be ignored—there are plenty of other errors that creep into polls that aren't reflected in the margin of error. When polls go spectacularly wrong, the problem is almost never caused by statistical error. A more insidious kind of error—systematic error—is almost always to blame. However, systematic errors are never included in a poll's margin of error. When journalists use the margin of error as a litmus test to figure out whether or not to believe a poll, they are completely blind to the sources of error that are most likely to render their poll meaningless. Every time a journalist cites the margin of error as a reason to believe the

section 6.2.2 "The quantitative analysis process provides an objective and empirical basis regarding risk potential." Just because a number is involved, that does not alone justify its classification as 'objective'. We have seen in the Challenger story how management and engineers could not come to an agreement on how to interpret the same information.

So, for a summary of this chapter, we began with showing how we subconsciously substitute a difficult question for an easier one. We followed that with the 'Tom' experiment that emphasized how difficult it is to neglect information that is irrelevant. Just because the judge tells us to ignore certain information, enough of it remains to affect our judgment. This was reinforced in the doctor/lawyer experiment where base rates were only used as a last resort.

We spent some time with patternicity which emphasizes our need to explain things. In the ski disaster story, we saw examples of Group Think at work with the bias to believe combining for a lethal decision. The availability heuristic was introduced to explain some of our estimates of probability. The availability heuristic begins with the belief that 'because it is frequent, it should be easy to access, and changes to 'because it is easy to access it occurs frequently.' There are a number of ways this can go wrong.

In chapter 4, we will see how many of these same rules of thumb, primarily regarding emotions and fear of regret, work against our ability to change when it would appear strongly advisable to do so.

---

results of a poll, he's doing the logical equivalent of looking only one way before crossing a two-way street. Sooner rather than later, he'll be clobbered by a bus."

Mumpsimus:

A traditional notion that is obstinately retained despite being unreasonable; a person who adheres to such a notion

A person who obstinately adheres to old ways in spite of clear evidence that they are wrong; an ignorant and bigoted opponent of reform. n. An obvious error that is obstinately repeated despite correction.

Mumpsimus is us.

Chapter 4

IRRATIONAL PERSEVERANCE: WHY IT'S SO HARD TO CHANGE OUR MINDS

Man is a credulous animal, and must believe
something; in the absence of good grounds for
belief, he will be satisfied with bad ones.
Bertrand Russell

Man's most valuable trait is a judicious
sense of what not to believe.
Euripides

The difficulty lies not so much in developing
new ideas as in escaping from old ones.
John Maynard Keynes

"The mind, once expanded to the dimensions of
larger ideas, never returns to its original size."
Oliver Wendell Holmes

"The human understanding when it has once adopted an
opinion draws all things else to support and agree with it. And
though there be a greater number and weight of instances to
be found on the other side, yet these it either neglects and
despises, or else by some distinction sets aside and rejects, in
order that by this great and pernicious predetermination the
authority of its former conclusion may remain inviolate."
Francis Bacon

"Do not quench your inspiration and your imagination;
do not become the slave of your model."
Vincent van Gogh

The man who views the world at 50 the same as
he did at 20 has wasted 30 years of his life.
Muhammad Ali

The door of a bigoted mind opens outward so that the only
result of the pressure of facts upon it is to close it more snugly.
Ogden Nash

Change is difficult. When it does happen, we can be almost
humorous in our efforts to deny it. Even when we have
information that should cause us to reconsider our beliefs,
we usually find ways to re-interpret it in ways that support
our beliefs. If change is too difficult, deny anything that
supports it.

The following three cases can also be looked at as
questionable conclusions to based on silent evidence (See
chap 5 under "what you don't know . . .") The more time
that passes without anything happening the more we think
it is due to occur, while it may be the opposite that is true.

An example from Trivers, pg 153,

> "President Franklin Roosevelt uprooted hundreds of thousands of Japanese-American citizens and interned them for the remainder of the World War II, all based on anticipation of possible disloyalty for which no evidence was ever produced except the following classic from a US general: "The very fact that no sabotage has taken place is a disturbing and confirming indication that such action *will* be taken." The General found an argument to lower his cognitive dissonance between his belief that an attack will happen and the negative, silent evidence that it is has not.

Or Schulz, pg 128,

> "The Iraq War also provides a nice example of another form of confirmation bias. At a point when conditions on the ground were plainly deteriorating, then-President George W. Bush argued otherwise by, in the words of the journalist George Packer, "interpreting increased violence in Iraq as a token of the enemy's frustration with American success." Sometimes, as Bush showed, we look straight at the counterevidence yet conclude that it supports our beliefs instead.

Or Shultz, pg 248,

> "A victim believed the accused to have been the true perpetrator. After hearing 16 different witnesses testify that the accused was at work that day, she . . . dismissed their stories as too similar

to each other to be believable—an outstanding example of interpreting the evidence against your theory as evidence for your theory."

Taleb Black pg 144 "The problem is that our ideas are sticky: once we produce a theory, we are not likely to change our minds—so those who delay developing their theories are better off. When you develop your opinions on the basis of weak evidence, you will have difficulty interpreting subsequent information that contradicts these opinions, even if this new information is obviously more accurate. Two mechanisms are at play here: the confirmation bias and belief perseverance, the tendency to not reverse opinions you already have. Remember that we treat ideas like possessions, and it will be hard for us to part with them."

Overconfidence, Patternicity, and Cognitive Ease

"No problem in judgment and decision making is more prevalent and more potentially catastrophic than overconfidence."[151] "Convictions are more dangerous enemies of truth than lies."[152] This chapter will look at some of the factors that can work against us changing our beliefs when we are presented with evidence that should convince us to do so. A few examples of the role of overconfidence in easing our decisions will illustrate some of the biases underlying our thinking when it goes wrong. We have already seen how System 1 gut feeling type of thinking is mostly hidden from our conscious, yet 'we', System 2, have to work with it to rationalize the beliefs and decisions that are made based on those feelings. "Reason is slave to

---

[151] Scott Plous, cited by Evans, pg 2
[152] Friedrich Wilhelm Nietzsche, philosopher (1844-1900)

the passions."[153] A case of the tail [emotion] wagging the [reason] dog?

Shermer writes,[154] "Beliefs come first, explanations for beliefs follow." Beliefs start as S1 phenomena, occasionally followed by evaluations of them in the S2 domain. He continues; "The brain is a belief engine. From sensory data flowing in through the senses the brain naturally begins to look for and find patterns, and then infuses those patterns with meaning." Beliefs are a result of our perception of the patterns and the stories we make to justify them. As the belief in a pattern is reinforced, sometimes from a lucky sequence of events, sometimes from the urging of friends, family, church, or political party, they become increasingly validated as true for the believer. Along this progression of increasing degrees of belief, some graduate to the level of faith,[155] a place where change is an unwelcomed stranger. Here, among other missteps, we elevate the risk of confusing correlations with causations. We seldom question our faith, and we fail to heed the admonishments that a belief which leaves no place for doubt is not a belief; it is a superstition.

Most of the time this interaction with the unconscious works fine, but if we don't want to be deceived we will need to be aware of the unconscious shortcuts we're biased to make. Also, if our beliefs are based on emotion and not on rational deliberation, new information that should affect our beliefs may not do so if it doesn't first change the source of our feelings.

Trivers wrote "Though people in general are overconfident regarding the truth of their assertions,

153   David Hume
154   Shermer Pg 5
155   "Believe those who are seeking truth, doubt those who find it."
      Andre Gide

narcissists are especially so."[156] They present especially good examples of stubbornly held beliefs, by displaying a notable reluctance to consider their own faults. They are less likely to learn from their mistakes because making mistakes is not something they associate their own actions with. By believing they are the chosen children, humility loses the battle with overconfidence for the reflection needed to know yourself. The favored ones fool themselves more than they fool others.

Patternicity and Belief

The tendency to look for patterns (patternicity) and form beliefs is based on a pattern's utility in supporting the predictions that are part of our survival tool kit. In the distant past, those who were better at it were more likely to be survived by their offspring. Those who weren't, not so much. Part of 'being better at it' includes being biased to find and act on patterns as having causes other than random noise, as opposed to not assigning any particular significance to the stimuli of our environment. If the pattern you find is chimerical, failure is just a learning experience. If you interpreted the movement in the bush as a bear, but were wrong, there is no problem. Contrast this with your interpreting a movement in the bush as nothing more than a random breeze. This time if you're wrong, the scorecard reads: Bear one, You zero.

By 'belief' I mean to indicate the expectations based on learning that the experiences of correlations, causations, and coincidences can lead us to have. If this, expect that. This is associative learning, and when associations are

---

[156] "If a man shall begin with certainties he will end in doubts, but if he be content to begin with doubts, he shall end in certainties." Francis Bacon.

repeatedly reinforced, like Pavlov's dog, we learn what to expect, what to believe[157]. With repetition comes familiarity, and with familiarity, a sense of knowing, a sense of conviction[158],[159] that is hard to change. With repetition, our neural connections strengthen and our feelings change from doubt, to assuredness. At this point, right or wrong, we find the benefits of cognitive ease, a primary goal for many of our decisions. We act on this sense of knowing the truth that familiarity brings, by dialing down the skepticism control and replacing uncomfortable uncertainty with habits and heuristics that generally ease our minds. Both habits and heuristics are handy because they are quick, don't require much thought, and are useful in achieving simplification. Because they don't require much thought, we are usually unaware of their existence. It's hard to change what is unknown.

---

[157] K&T 164 "That associative bonds are strengthened by repetition is perhaps the oldest law of memory known to man. The availability heuristic exploits the inverse form of this law, that is, it uses strength of association as a basis for the judgment of frequency." Pavlov's dog associated a bell with the appearance of food. As the two events became associated, the bell could cause salivation in anticipation of food. The firing together of neurons for detection of savory odors and tasty food becomes an association as it is repeated over time, and eventually the firing of the odor neurons leads to the firing of the food neuron. Simply put, "Neurons that fire together wire together." (Hebb's Law)

[158] "Convictions are more dangerous enemies of truth than lies." -Friedrich Wilhelm Nietzsche, philosopher (1844-1900)

[159] pg 87 of K2011. ". . . participants who saw one-sided evidence were more confident of their judgments than those who saw both sides. This is just what you would expect if the confidence that people experience is determined by the coherence of the story they manage to construct from available information. It is the consistency of the information that matters for a good story, not its completeness."

Simplification by imprecision feels good and allows us to process information quickly. A list of the Fightin' Phillies final scores may facilitate your speed in evaluation of their performance better if the list also includes a simple 'W' or 'L' for each game, or a summary count of wins and losses.

Trust or belief in a number increases with the precision of that number.[160] This can be shown by experiments in which adjustments, departures, and recalibrations of anchors tend to be less when the numbers are highly precise. There is implicitly more uncertainty, less information in rounded, imprecise numbers. This is a carryover from the world of anecdotes where greater information in the form of precise details, allow us to better imagine and remember. The detail in stories, even if wrong, makes us feel we are familiar with the story, so we question it less, trust it more. The same goes for numbers. Although the anchor may be of high precision, that doesn't mean it is of high accuracy, though that would be a reasonable expectation. While we would not want to interfere with adjustments to accuracy which understated precision encourages, we do need to take a second look at the reliability of a number's accuracy and precision before burying its information in the dust bins of simplified, rounded results.[161]

If you are analyzing measurements to determine which of two processes is more capable of producing good product, it will require more measurements to make a decision with the same degree of confidence if you have previously simplified the data by excessive rounding of original results. Even worse than oversimplification by over rounding is the practice of changing variable data to pass / fail attribute data. These practices lose essential

---

[160] Herbert pg 123
[161] "Get your facts first, then you can distort them as much as you please." Mark Twain

information, and unfortunately are sometimes employed
with the hope of purposely losing enough information
to arrive at a predetermined decision such as; 'there is
insufficient information to determine whether a statistically
significant difference exists.' If you don't want data to
indicate a difference, get rid of some of the information
in the data. This is what NASA did when it excluded good
O-ring performance at high temperatures.

Simplification has its place. "As much as you believe
in the "keep-it-simple-stupid", it is the simplification that
is dangerous."[162] We've almost all simplified one behavior
by committing it to the auto control of the unconscious;
walking. Once infants learn to overcome the difficulty of
their first wobbly steps, they simplify life by delegating the
mental control of walking to the unconscious (S1) brain.
This is an example of, for this particular skill, practice
making perfect enough to achieve the cognitive ease that
comes from not having fallen down in a while. You don't
even have to think about it, you could do it in your sleep.
Nevertheless, when needed, like when hiking a rocky path
up a mountain or crossing a shallow stream, we can still
bring the rational conscious mind to bear on a normally S1
task and focus on how to negotiate obstacles.

Predictability should be a strong test of the validity
of belief. This begs the question, when a belief fails to
predict, do we change the belief, or do we explain away the
outcome?

When our expectations are not met, we may experience
the anxiety of being wrong. If it's a big error like believing
a marriage would be forever, we may start to doubt our
decision making prowess in general. When this happens
we adjust our beliefs or perceptions as experience dictates
to get back to cognitive ease. We learn to believe a new
reality. Or at least that is how it is supposed to work in

---

[162]   Taleb xlvi

theory. As Yogi Berra supposedly said, "In theory, there is no difference between theory and practice. In practice, there is." This disjunction of what beliefs we should change and why we do not, has many causes and often leads to the question, 'What *were* we thinking?'.

Learning to believe . . . . and disbelieve?

When learning occurs over a suitable frequency and time span, long term memory becomes established. The establishment of beliefs is brought about in a similar way. If we can accept that a belief is a learned response, it is tempting to think that beliefs take time to be created and time to disappear because they follow the same process that long term memory requires: synaptic restructuring. Long term memory is a physical state associated with structural changes in the neuronal pathways such as increased number of pre-synaptic terminals. These terminals can be increased by sensitization and retracted back into the neuron by the process of habituation. The stronger the synaptic transmission the more difficult and longer it will take to unlearn. Disbelieving, a requirement for changing beliefs, isn't easy. It's not who we are.

I wonder, if we need to think about the belief in order to change it, might we be creating our own resistance to change? Just thinking about the belief may in and of itself promote neuronal strengthening, just the opposite of what we are trying to do. If you are told to NOT THINK of something, like the scratch on the driver's side door of your car, what are you now imagining? Probably the scratch on the driver's side door of your car. Substitute belief for the car scratch and we have another reason why it's so hard to deliberately unlearn. From the 2013 Jan/Feb issue of Scientific American Mind, Lilienfield references studies that show that a judge's admonition to the jury to disregard (dawnevintinkabowdit) certain pieces of evidence falls on deaf ears. As easy as it is to forget from neglect deliberately trying to forget is not easy to do.

The difficulty in changing beliefs is a direct product of the difficulty of trying to simultaneously hold two dissonant ideas in the mind in order to unlearn what we previously thought was true. "The difficulty lies not so much in developing new ideas as in escaping from old ones." John Maynard Keynes

How do we learn? By our experiences mostly. Whether it be that eating satisfies hunger, or that the association of touching a hot stove with the resulting pain teaches us to look before we leap, there first must be some stimulus to our senses that we can associate with a reaction. Learning is evidenced as a change in behavior due to experience. Experience is our best teacher, and perhaps this is true because first she gives us the test, and then the lesson. And lessons should, as Alice was to learn in Wonderland, lessen over time. But I digress.

It would obviously be more efficient and evolutionarily favored not to have to start from scratch every time we need to react to a situation that we have experienced in the past. There should be some memory, conscious or not, that we can take advantage of to guide our behavior. We come into this world with a memory that is hardwired to help us get started with the basics. This memory is essentially the lessons our ancestors learned. It puts us on the right path to using our biological software, neuronal plasticity, to learn our own lessons.

The adjustment or change in beliefs is an adjustment in expectations, based in memory. Dopamine neurons will decrease their synaptic strength if there is a failure to predict, if an association fails to happen. To over simplify, whatever ups the neurotransmitter dopamine (DA) flow beyond the expected, will be associated with something that makes us feel good. More DA, below a certain limit where schizophrenia may occur, makes us feel good and makes us want to repeat the thing that caused the additional DA. On the other hand, when the predicted DA is less than the expected, expect some degree of emotional distress such as fear.

Just like Goldilocks weighing in on the ideal porridge temperature, we want our DA levels just right, not too much, not too little.

DA is one of the brain's chemical currencies, or as I like to think of it, its funny money. Shermer calls it the belief drug. It is the principle neurotransmitter associated with reward and pleasure. In 1954 Olds and Miller found that when the rat's NAcc (nucleus accumbens) was stimulated by a constant electrical current, the production of dopamine was so great that they would cease normal eating and feeding behavior. Within a few days they died of thirst. Too much of a good thing, or as Bob Dylan put it, "Money doesn't talk, it swears." The self-medication of cocaine operates in this same neuronal dialogue. This drug alters the synaptic molecular conversation by interfering with the re-uptake of dopamine by the presynaptic neurons that had been stimulated to release it. The dopamine thus becomes more available to the postsynaptic neurons with the resulting high. The postsynaptic neuron can adjust and make more receptors to accommodate the increased availability of DA. When this happens and use of the drug is stopped, the unmet demands of the increased number of receptors results in cravings and depression. When an experience fails the test of predictability, DA neurons put the brakes on dopamine secretion. If the S1 expectations are not met, S2 is physiologically alerted to the situation and it responds to the uncomfortable feelings. The misbalance of supply and demand is felt and eventually returned to equilibrium.

"The connection between DA and belief was established by experiments conducted by Perer Bruger and his colleague Christie Mohr at the University of Bristol in England. Exploring the neurochemistry of superstition, magical thinking, and belief in the paranormal, Brugger and Mohr found that people with high levels of dopamine are more likely to find significance in coincidences and pick out meaning and patterns where there are none."[163] When L-Dopa, which is converted to dopamine in the brain, is used to treat Parkinson's disease, some patients with their elevated sense of pattern finding, become compulsive gamblers. Dopamine affects learning by enhancing the ability of neurons to transmit signals between one another. It increases the rate of neural firing in association with pattern recognition. One might ask the question as to whether this activity of dopamine has the purpose of promoting Type 1 errors (such as believing something happened when it didn't, witnessed by an overly eager openness to detect patterns) which I argue elsewhere is evolutionarily preferable to Type 2 errors (believing nothing happened when it did).

Overconfidence and Cognitive Ease

Why do opinions and beliefs hold us as much as we hold them? Why is changing these ideas and beliefs so hard to do? Overconfidence for one. Overconfidence could be said to be the confidence that you sometimes have before you fully understand the situation. It is associated with the sensation of knowing, and that is a happy, uncritical place to be. This overconfidence may be in ourselves or it might be in those to whom we have passed a particular decision making responsibility. We may simplify our lives by deferring to our religious leaders or delegating to a team member. If they don't change, neither do we.

---

[163] Shermer pg 118/119

If we expect our level of confidence that we know the truth to match the true probability that we actually do know the truth, we will be disappointed. We are pretty sure of stuff that just ain't so, and unaware of what we do not know.

Poor estimates of margin of error demonstrate that we are usually more confident than the information merits. While we might think of overconfidence as arrogance, it is often a little more nuanced than that. Sometimes we just don't have enough information to make a good estimate, and the greater problem is that we may not even know that this missing information is missing. Despite the problems overconfidence fosters, we expect experts to display a high degree of it. Politicians, teachers, doctors are expected to be confident, and not to voice uncertainty. "An unbiased appreciation of uncertainty is a cornerstone of rationality— but it is not what people and organizations want."[164]

An example: Studies[165] at Duke University collected data over several years where CFOs were asked to estimate the returns of the Standard & Poor's index for the following year. They were asked to construct a confidence interval around their estimates by giving a number that they were 90% sure was too high, and a number that they were 90% sure was too low. If these numbers were accurate, the expectation would be that 20% of the actual results would be outside of this interval. What actually happened was that almost 70% of the actual results were outside their expectations. Their overconfidence, as evidenced in margin of error, was too optimistic, too assured. Recall Feynman's question, why *do* we believe in unsupported probabilities? Similar experiments are consistent with the conclusion of this one: while it serves to assuage our need for certainty, overconfidence is to be found among unfounded or wrong beliefs, and that can translate into unfounded or wrong

---

[164] K2011 pg 263.
[165] K2011 pg 261-2

decisions. Why we remain so overconfident in the face of error is an important query, some answers to which we will explore in the following pages. Other biases and their associated heuristics will also be looked at for their role in keeping us glued to the status quo.

Overconfidence in the Court Room.

Consider a witness faced with a simultaneous line-up of suspects. If we choose the one that has an appearance close to the actual criminal, we will be more likely to believe we have chosen well, while at the same time will more likely be wrong[166] than if a sequential lineup was being evaluated. For this reason, the use of simultaneous suspect lineups is decreasing in favor of one at a time (sequential) suspect lineups.

Myside Bias

"We are usually convinced more easily by reasons we have found ourselves than by those which have occurred to others."—Blaise Pascal, philosopher and mathematician (1623-1662). This is an example of myside bias, where we find a way to make ourselves always appear to be right. If

---

[166] SciAmMind Jan/Feb 2013 pg 50. Another case of changing the question. When presented with a lineup, we ask ourselves the question, 'who, amongst these suspects, is the most likely to have been seen at the crime?' although the question was 'Were any of these suspects at the scene of the crime?' This relative kind of thinking leads to a higher likelihood of choosing someone, and so more often a wrong identification follows. In a sequential lineup we would be asking, 'who is the person seen at the crime?' The use of a sequential lineup promotes absolute over relative thinking.

Hardy is convinced that he is intellectually superior to Laurel, he finds a way to take the credit when Laurel comes up with a good idea. "You're actually using your brain. That comes from associating with me."[167] We take credit where none is due, and then there is the flip side, where we blame any errors we made on someone else.

If you are in the process of justifying your beliefs, the end result is your result, your creation, and our personal creations are held and defended dearly. This is part of the narrative of overconfidence and another reason to not change.

"When he [Winnie the Pooh] plots to eat honey from the bees' nest, he realizes that bees don't much like bears, and so masquerades as a black rain cloud. A disguise? Certainly. One that is likely to fool bees? Perhaps not. But when the bees fail to be taken in, becoming "suspicious" of the little rain cloud hovering by their nest, Pooh's immediate reaction is not that his choice of costume was a bad one, but rather that he is dealing with "*the wrong sort of bees.*"[168] It's not me; it's you . . . .

Fine wrote[169] "Our sensitivity to context, so sharply tuned when we apply it to ourselves, becomes sloppy and careless when we focus on others." We find wrong doing by another person to more likely indicate a failure of character than due to associated circumstances. Our own cargoes are delayed due to the choppy seas of circumstance rather than our own misdoings. Other people's ships sail into

---

[167]   the movie, Pardon Us. 1931

[168]   (http://blogs.scientificamerican.com/literally-psyched/2011/12/28/winnie-the-pooh-and-the-pervasiveness-of-egocentric-bias-why-we-are-all-that-sort-of-bear/?WT_mc_id=SA_DD_20111229 (from Maria Konnikova, a writer living in New York City, is a doctoral candidate in Psychology at Columbia University Lyterally Psyched Scientific American Blog)

[169]   Fine pg 65

harbor late because of their dillydallying. This practice of blaming other's errors on faults of their character rather than on context, external forces, is another way of exalting our overly confidant opinions of ourselves, leaving us self satisfied, which works against any motivation to change.

The generally positive view of ourselves is so pervasive that when faced with the rapid response as to which of two letters in a pair of letters is the most attractive, we mostly choose letters from our own names. Even more so we choose the initials of our first or last names. Our need for CE is pervasive, and that need is fed by familiarity. What's more familiar to you than you?

When we make a decision, we overestimate how many others would make the same decision as we would—the consensus bias. And we don't stop there. We also overweight the importance of our own experiences and underweight those of others. Our own starting perspective is the spotlight effect (everyone is watching me). We are slower to indicate another's perception would be different from, rather than similar to, our own.[170] Egocentric anchoring and adjustment means that even when we try to change our decisions in the direction of others, we fall short, remaining closer to our own anchor. And that, perhaps, is the most disturbing part of the story: we may all truly want to understand the Heffalump's (from Winnie the Pooh) preferences[171] but try as we might, our understanding will begin and end with ourselves. We defend our beliefs of who we are. We construct and reconstruct the world around us so that we don't have to change. I'm ok, the world's wrong.

---

[170] Journal of Personality and Social Psychology 2004, Vol. 87 No. 3, 327-339 Epley et. Al.

[171] On their quest to catch a Heffalump, Piglet and Pooh fail to agree on the best bait for the Very Big Pit that will serve as the Cunning Trap for the mysterious beast. But when discussing what food to lure the Heffalump into a trap, we tend to suggest food we like, not necessarily the food the Heffalump likes.

Cognitive Ease and its opposite: Fear

One of the signposts that will guide us in this quest for why it is so hard to change is the understanding that we're motivated to reduce stress and reach a state of cognitive ease. We're hedonists. Cognitive ease is the state of being that results from an environment where there is a sense of familiarity, a feeling of control (even if it is an illusion of control), zero threats. Happy Land. The advantages of being in this condition include the ability to free our minds enough to use our imaginations to solve less urgent and more complex problems. There are also the health advantages of being happy (cognitive ease leads to immunological[172] enhancement and heart health) that overconfidence supports by reducing stress. The positive relation of overconfidence and stress reduction is a strong one. It's a nice feeling to at least think you know what's happening.

The principle task of the brain has been to survive, which has always been more important than the secondary task of knowing the truth. If it takes some irrational, truth defying decisions to survive, we will take the tradeoff of behaving irrationally. We see this all too often in political campaigns. Politicians tell you things that are not necessarily what they believe, in order to encourage you to vote for their political survival. Truth is the first victim of stress, and it will be sacrificed where it interferes with survival. For example, it may seem somewhat irrational to be happy and hopeful, expecting to win the lottery, believing in things getting better when you are living on the street. That is, unless you contrast that seeming irrationality with the same situation but where hopelessness is brought

---

[172] Trivers pg 122 "Likewise [testosterone], corticosteroids—produced in response to stress and associated with anxiety and fear—are immune suppressors."

on by a rational expectation of a bleak future. That's a hard way to go. More stress due to the rational realization that things are unlikely to get better has little evolutionary advantage. Better to accentuate the positive.

Decisions are rational as far as they help us achieve our goals, not necessarily because they are logical. Ignorance of the truth of our condition does not always lead to irrational decisions. Irrational beliefs can have real adaptive benefits—from the placebo effect to a sense of hope in tough situations. If rational thinking were to be defined as whatever leads to happiness, we might well have to change our view of what rational thinking is. Instead of respect of evidence, neglect of evidence might turn out to be effective and rational.

A Dilbert cartoon plays on the delicate balance between being in and out of cognitive bliss.

Ratbirt is talking to Dilbert, "I may be an ignorant rat, but that's okay because ignorance is . . . um . . . um . . . ,

Dilbert: "Bliss . . . Ignorance is Bliss",

Ratbirt "Oh, great. Now it's gone"

Dilbert "oops".

The rat's feeling of well being rests, much like many heuristics, on lack of information or on simplification.

Congnitive ease comes with a price. For example, in order to lower the stress related to having to make a decision, we unconsciously employ our little helpers, the heuristics. When we make the decision with the help of a biased heuristic, we may become overconfident with our rationalization, not realizing that we are making a deal with the devil that trades quickness for accuracy. As per Wyatt Earp's observation on showdowns, "Fast is fine, but accuracy is everything." Understanding of how we know what we know must take into consideration the contradictory nature of thought's reward systems. The feeling of knowing, the reward for both proven and unproven thoughts, is learning's best friend and mental flexibility's worst enemy.

Whatever makes a decision easier, such as using the affect heuristic to dumb down and simplify by skipping the analytical in favor of going with our feelings, also reduces the uneasy feelings such as fear.[173] This was probably was even truer for our distant ancestors, as their daily life and death decisions needed to be made, often instinctively, quickly, without sufficient information. Can I eat this plant? Is this visitor friendly? Is that a bear in the bush? Should I stay or should I go? Heuristics of the day might have been, eat what others eat, distrust those that do not look like you, assume the worst with predators, and stop to observe, otherwise move on. Getting a solution, any solution, can help calm our minds for the moment, at least until we see if the solution works.

Fear stimulated alertness was natural for our forebears, as it was vital to their survival. We still carry the machinery of fear into the decision making process. We shouldn't feel fear when deciding to purchase a car, but our aversion to loss, the possibility of regret for not making a different

---

[173] Burton pg 28 . . .the amygdala-long known to be crucial to the recognizing, processing, and remembering of emotional reactions, including the fear response. Note in the following that reducing 3 choices to 2 with a decoy results in less fear.

Ariely pg 10 You have to choose between a vacation package in Paris or Rome. Similar costs, similar attractions. A tough call until you add a third option that was the same as for Rome, but without the free breakfast. Now the original Rome package is looking better than the Rome package without the free breakfast, so good that it is now favored over the Paris package. The decoy didn't have a chance of being favored, but it gave a bump to the Rome package. As Ariely would say, not rational, but predictable.

The uncomfortable feeling of having to make a difficult decision in order to reduce ambiguity is due to a fear response. The fear may be based on the dread of regret.

Burton pg 29 . . . bilateral removal of the amygdala in animals, from rats to monkeys, produces a state of utter fearlessness.

choice, feels like fear. Fear of the regret of being wrong acts as a brake to our impulses. Fear of regret is not such a big concern among the overconfident. Overconfidence creeps in when we don't have all the information because we don't know that we don't have all the information[174]. Why measure twice before cutting? Like gamblers, they will take credit for the successes and write off the failures as due to conditions beyond their control and/or due to someone else. This resulting overconfidence and subsequent fearlessness exposes the individual to risky behavior, which may lead to a gold pot or to a cold plot. The cost of achieving cognitive ease includes the cost of employing heuristics and living with their biased results. Since we are unaware of these heuristically generated biases, we may not recognize the errors they cause. Voila, cognitive ease and overconfidence in harmony. Ignorance is bliss.

From Taleb Fool xlii (prologue) ". . . we may enjoy presenting conjectures as truth. It is our nature." We fool to rule. If it takes a conjecture to be disguised as truth to reduce ambiguity, it will be rewarded with cognitive ease.

How the Affect Heuristic leads us to resist change

Sometimes to decide to not change is the easiest, simplistic option.[175]. This "no decision" more generally refers to not changing from the default, whether or not the default is an action.[176] Suppose the default decision was

---

[174] "We know accurately only when we know little, with knowledge doubt increases." Goethe

[175] Not changing can lead to the Buriden's donkey problem, where the donkey can't decide which of two food sources it should choose, and so does not eat at all. The inability to choose a change supports the status quo.

[176] If we want everything to remain as it is, it will be necessary for everything to change. Guisepe Tomasi di Lampadusa

the action of following the standard practice of ordering a certain expensive diagnostic test for a particular set of symptoms. In this case, it will be a cause for great anxiety if we err in deciding against the default and do not test, when it is found later that the patient's problem could have been diagnosed by performing the test. On the other hand, the anxiety of committing the error of deciding to not change and do the costly test when the results were unnecessary would be less. In this case, the asymmetric nature of the risk/benefit outcome for errors favors not changing from the accepted practice. "The physician who prescribes the unusual treatment faces a substantial risk of regret, blame, and perhaps litigation. True, a good outcome will contribute to the reputation of the physician who dared, but the potential benefit is smaller than the potential cost."[177]

Taleb writes[178] "Our neglect of silent evidence [what doesn't happen, lives not lost] kills people daily. Assume that a drug saves many people from a potentially dangerous ailment, but runs the risk of killing a few, with a net benefit to society. Would a doctor prescribe it? He has no incentive to do so. The lawyers of the person hurt by the side effects will go after the doctor like attack dogs, while the lives saved by the drug might not be accounted for anywhere. A life saved is a statistic; a person hurt is an anecdote. Statistics are invisible; anecdotes are salient."

The reason that it is often easier to do nothing is that, when things go south, we feel less anxiety when it was caused by our inaction than when caused by our action. Consider the following two, almost equivalent, scenarios. In the first, you are driving a trolley. The brakes have failed and you have a choice: continue on track which would kill a group of five workers, or change to tracks where there is

---

[177] K2011, pg 349
[178] Taleb Black, pg 112

only one person who will be killed. Compare this with the same train without brakes but this time you are an observer, and you have a chance to push a large man onto the tracks to stop the trolley. What do you do? In the first scenario most likely you will choose to change tracks, but in the second, most of us feel a greater unease that comes with the up close and personal pushing of this man to his death. An in-between option is that you could open a trap door and let him fall to his death. The first scenario puts some space and time between your action and the resulting death of one person. The cause of our feelings might be more closely associated with how we did what we did than what we actually did. Emotions are part of our decisions.

Another example shows how feelings depend more on the context or history of how a situation is arrived at than the actual situation. From Kahneman[179]:

> "Paul owns shares in company A. During the past year he considered switching to stock in company B, but he decided against it. He now learns that he would have been better off by $1,200 if he had switched to the stock of company B."

> "George owned shares in company B. During the past year he switched to stock in company A. He now learns that he would have been better off by $1,200 if he he'd kept his stock in company B."

Who feels greater regret? Respondents said George 92% of the time. Both men would have been better off going or staying with B, but both actively or inactively finished with A. George's activity lead to more regret than Paul's inactivity although both of their decisions resulted in the same cost. In this case, not changing meant less regret.

---

[179]   K2011, pg 348

In another experiment using a computer simulation, black jack players were asked one of the two questions, "do you want to hit?", or "Do you wish to stand?" In either case, if the outcome was bad, saying yes was associated with much more regret than answering no. It is the departure from the default, which was your last call (hit or stand), that produces greater regret.

These situations all point to the potential feelings of regret as a reason to raise the likelihood of preferring inaction to action. All things equal, we prefer to stay with what we have been doing or the standard way of doing things so that we resist change. An object at rest remains at rest until . . . .

No matter how far you've gone down the wrong road, turn back. Don't allow belief to become a mental habit, thinking the same, thinking the same, irrationally persevering. "The door of a bigoted mind opens outward so that the only result of the pressure of facts upon it is to close it more snugly." Ogden Nash. The bigoted mind does not welcome information that challenges its comfortable overconfident beliefs. Consistency feels good, so unless rewarded for breaking with the same old same old . . . we prefer to not change.

How is overconfidence maintained in the face of dissonance?

Here we go with the excuses.

Do we resist change due to its costing us extra mental work to think through the new information to determine if this is the best course? Is it because changing course might actually be a bad idea? Does it have to do with the stress (expectation of regret) of being wrong? Is it because we are so sure of ourselves that we don't see the need for change? Yes, yes, yes, and yes.

Despite all the above bad mouthing of overconfidence, it has some positive evolutionary implications. Progress owes much to those who took risks that required a high level of fearless confidence. We learn from our own mistakes and those of others. More mistakes caused by more risky behavior would be suspected of as being more common among the overconfident, so it follows that learning can be an upside of overconfidence. Overconfidence is evolutionarily maintained even though it's a risky business. That said, the following is a series of generally unconscious elements that work against our ability to turn on a dime, our ability to change away from biased decision making and beliefs.

We overvalue the beliefs that we are overconfident in: The Endowment effect can be summarized as the bias you have to stay with your current beliefs and material things and unless you are paid more to part with them than it cost you to obtain them. This is related to the principles of loss aversion that state that a dollar received gives less pleasure than the regret of a dollar lost. To get a sense of this feeling, ask yourself if you would accept a proposition of betting $100 based on a coin flip. Gaining $100 would be nice, but the feeling of losing $100 is worse than the good feeling of gaining $100. You pass on the gamble, keep the $100 and stay with the status quo. Again, because you are averse to taking the risk of losing, you are biased to stay with what you have, including your opinions and beliefs. When we change a belief, it can feel like we are a different person. When our beliefs are challenged, it can feel like an insult. If we act on our beliefs and err, we can expect the snide, 'What *were* you thinking?' Changing your mind means losing part of who you are, and that loss needs to be compensated for. The pride of rejecting change because of the "not invented here" effect adds to the cost of giving up on your ownership.

Cognitive dissonance is the uncomfortable feeling you get when there is a conflict between the judgment of need for change and a contrary prior feeling or belief. Our attempt to resolve the conflict will require less work to defend the belief you have previously chosen and are committed to, than to convert, so we are biased to not change.

An easily understood physical example of **Cognitive dissonance** is the experience of motion sickness. This is a result of a conflict between the type of motion being experienced—the unfamiliar pitch of a boat, and the type of motion vs. the more commonly expected solid, unmoving, ground.

Dissonance between two competing points of view is an uncomfortable state to be in. This stress, fear, or uneasiness will cause cognitive strain, and so is not at equilibrium. For the overconfident individual, once again this problem is diminished. Since his mind is already overly sure about what it believes, potentially dissonant information is barred from consideration and cognitive ease retained.

My-Side bias sounds a tad Machiavellian (or Ayn Randian?). The "Yo voy a mi" (a bumper sticker popular in the 1980s in Puerto Rico meaning I believe in myself, I'm betting on me, I'm going for me) attitude would favor your having more confidence in how you work for your self-interests vs. other's efforts towards your self-interests. You are not their top priority. They have their own problems. Each of us is the lead actor in the theater of life, and this perspective of being in the spot light can be a confidence builder. Believing in yourself runs contrary to changing your beliefs. You interpret results that conflict with your beliefs are as coming from flawed studies, rather than evidence that disproves your belief. 'Your criticism of my belief indicates a gap in your understanding.' Our fault is that we stick with the default, in spite of the dissonance.

Your Leadership and expertise may come into question if you decide that an old belief that you held was wrong and now deserves a change. Not changing can give the

appearance of confidence in yourself which is also rewarded
by others who see it as a sign of leadership or expertise.
This impression left on others comes back to us in the
form of adulation. Hey, if they think I'm right, who am I
to disagree? Another log on the fire of overconfidence. We
need to be aware that in these cases, overconfidence could
be so strongly self-serving that it may be confounded with
the illusion of degree of truth that is being proffered. I'm
only 50% sure, but I'll tell them I'm 100% sure. Assurance
of certainty sells well because it feels good, not because it is
correct. Some think that changing one's mind is a sign of
weakness and that a good thinker is one who is determined,
committed, and steadfast. With this belief, you may be more
likely to persist in irrational beliefs than make a change.
To repeat Taleb, "we may enjoy presenting conjectures
[opinions] as truth." There's a Dilbert cartoon where
Dilbert and Wally talk about expressing opinions.

Wally: "I like to have opinions, but not informed opinions.
It takes so much work to get informed that it defeats the
whole point of having an opinion in the first place."

Dilbert: "What exactly do you think is the "point" of having
an opinion"?

Wally: "The point is that it feels good."

Wally is a prime example of a hedonist. He has no
interest in working and will often do a great deal of work to
avoid it. As Lee Iacocca supposedly once said, "People want
economy and they are willing to pay any price to get it."

Confirmation bias[180] is the tendency to choose
information that is supportive of our beliefs and to ignore
non-confirming information, as expressed in the quote
by Bacon at the beginning of this chapter. Choosing what

---

[180] Taleb Black pg 55, "By a mental mechanism I call naïve
empiricism, we have a natural tendency to look for instances
that confirm and our story and our vision of the world—these
instances are always easy to find."

evidence is supportive is called a "positive test strategy."[181] The related congruence heuristic motivates us to look for results that would appear if a hypothesis is true.[182] We like explanations and stories that are cohesive and coherent. These practices that result in a reinforcement of our overconfident view of the world are another couple of nails in the coffin assuring our beliefs will prevail over the need to change. The Confirmation bias works to maintain current thinking instead of arguing for change. "No amount of [confirming] experimentation can ever prove me right; a single [disconfirming] experiment can prove me wrong." Albert Einstein. Confirming evidence does not test the hypothesis, disconfirming does. If disconfirming information is found, this sets up an uncomfortable, dissonant situation. Unconsciously aware of this, we avoid the stress of dissonance by not searching for contradictory evidence. Confirming evidence feeds confidence, feels good, and is so much less complicated.

Direct tests of hypotheses look for confirmation, while indirect tests disconfirmation, falsification.[183] The congruence bias states that we tend to look for confirmation more frequently than disconfirmation. Keep getting supporting information. Cognitive ease follows, change doesn't. It's hard to change because we test incorrectly, by looking to confirm instead of to disconfirm.

Unfortunately, this effort to disregard conflicting new information often leads to defensive behavior about one's own opinions and consequent replacement of reason by faith[184]. If you came to your beliefs by faith, reason will not

---

[181] K2011 pg 81 "A deliberate search for confirming evidence."
[182] Baron pg 171/173.
[183] Baron pg 172
[184] "Those who have the habit of revelation lose the habit of thought." Robin Skelton. We may have forgotten how we made our original decisions, so we don't know on what basis to

suffice to change those beliefs. "It is useless to attempt to reason a man out of a thing he was never reasoned into."— Jonathan Swift, satirist (1667-1745) Taleb Black pg xxxi "You need a story to displace a story. Metaphors and stories are far more potent (alas) than ideas; they are also easier to remember and more fun to read."

Memories of that seen at the scene . . . or was it?

Memories suffer from a variety of disabling interferences. We will argue that these impediments to memory are also impediments to change. Once upon a time not long ago, memory was thought to be like a movie, where all the information was there, waiting to be called upon. Now it is generally accepted that the process in retrieving a memory is a process of reconstruction.

This reconstruction tends to leave gaps, and these gaps are filled in with plausible guesses that are often just not true. We remember things that didn't even happen and forget what did. As well, our memories of the event can't help being influenced by knowledge of events that have happened since. Memories are also linked to the environment in which the memory was formed. Testing that memory in a different environment will result in less accurate recall. Changes of our memories due to this reconstruction will tend to be biased in favor of our self-image. This aspect of memory works against change, as it gives you a chance to inflate your confidence more than is merited. Why would you undo that? Unflattering aspects of a memory create dissonance with our confidence. If you don't like the memory, your subconscious changes it or just

---

compare the old belief with the new one. We have faith that we were right the first time (myside bias.)

moves it offstage. The dissonance is dissipated and the need for change is no longer.

Memories are by necessity incomplete. While there are individuals with memory abilities that are off the chart, they often pay the price of getting so caught up in the details that generalizations and decision making become more difficult than you would expect from an average mind. If you can't decide, you can't change. On the other hand, an incomplete memory allows greater girth, that is, fewer restrictions on the resulting story we tell ourselves in order to continually convince ourselves "We're # 1".

Memories get jostled by associated events such as when, where, with whom, etc. If presented with the odor of fresh cut grass, you may associate and call up a certain pleasant sunny spring morning from years ago. When asked if you visited a museum in 2005, you might recall your last visit as being with a friend, who moved away from the area in 2005, and so your answer is maybe. Without the associations that support of your memory, you may not be able to be assured of your answer. Then you remember that the visit happened on a day when you also went to a new restaurant. You look up the restaurant, and find it opened for business December 2004. This helps but you look for more information. Now you remember that it was winter, a few days after a Shriner parade. We reconstruct our answers from memory, sometimes little by little.

In the 2013 Jan/Feb issue of Scientific Mind, Scott O. Lilienfield writes: "Believing is our default state, so it comes to us naturally; disbelieving does not." It's easier to imagine something happening than something not happening. Compare the ease of imagining "He saw a white cat with a black ear" vs. "He did not see a white cat with a black ear." It's almost as if we have to, in the second case, imagine both possibilities so that we construct the visual of a particular cat as a criteria for what is not allowed to be imagined. This extra mental work to disbelieve favors our bias to believe, which can work against changing a belief. If we believe something happened, our selective memory will work to maintain that belief. This bias to believe is consistent with the bias to make Type 1 decision errors.

Scott also wrote a commentary in the November 2010 Scientific American Magazine[185] on the possible use of the confirmation basis by a Harvard University professor.

> "As of this writing, the precise nature of Marc Hauser's transgressions remains murky. Hauser is Harvard's superstar primate psychologist—and, perhaps ironically, an expert on the evolution of morality—whom the university recently found guilty of eight counts of scientific misconduct. Harvard has kept mum about the details, but a former lab assistant alleged that when Hauser looked at videotapes of rhesus monkeys, in an experiment on their capacity to learn sound patterns, he noted behavior that other people in the lab couldn't see, in a way that consistently favored his hypothesis. When confronted with these discrepancies, the assistant says, Hauser asserted imperiously that his interpretation was right and the others' wrong."

> "It's entirely possible that Hauser was swayed by "confirmation bias"—the tendency to look for and perceive evidence consistent with our hypotheses and to deny, dismiss or distort evidence that is not. Even the best and the brightest scientists can be swayed by it, especially when they are deeply invested in their own hypotheses and the data are ambiguous. Two

---

[185] http://www.scientificamerican.com/article.cfm?id=fudge-factor&WT.mc_id=SA_DD_20101215

factors make combating confirmation bias an uphill battle. For one, data show that eminent scientists tend to be more arrogant and confident than other scientists[186]. As a consequence, they may be especially vulnerable to confirmation bias and to wrong-headed conclusions, unless they are perpetually vigilant. Second, the mounting pressure on scholars to conduct single-hypothesis-driven research programs supported by huge federal grants is a recipe for trouble. Many scientists are highly motivated to disregard or selectively reinterpret negative results that could doom their careers. Yet when members of the scientific community see themselves as invulnerable to error, they impede progress and damage the reputation of science in the public eye. The very edifice of science hinges on the willingness of investigators to entertain the possibility that they might be wrong."[187]

Again, this imagining or remembering is biased to the gullible state of believing. If S2 gets overloaded, the default is S1, and S1 is not judgmental, it accepts what it experiences. S1 adheres to its mantra of, What You See Is

---

[186] Trivers pg 14. "A very disturbing feature of overconfidence is that it often appears to be poorly associated with knowledge— that is, the more ignorant the individual, the more confident he or she may be. Sometimes this phenomenon varies with age and status, so that senior physicians, for example, are both more likely to be wrong and more confident they are right."

[187] See Burton 167 for ""Good science is more than the mechanics of research and experimentation. Good science requires that scientists look inward to contemplate the origin of their thoughts. The failures of science do not begin with flawed evidence or fumbled statistics; they begin with personal self-deception and an unjustified *sense of knowing*."

All There Is (WYSIATI), so don't expect change unless S2 evaluates the input from S1. This is echoed with comedian Jerry Seinfeld's transparent answer to the question of what men are really thinking about, which was "nothing". WYSIATI.

Information subsequent to a particular event can affect the confidence of a memory of that event. That fact that the event turned out to be a win for Team A, might lead us to confidently say we knew all along it was going to happen. This assuredness doesn't coincide with our degree of confidence of a winning result the day before the game. Gambler's memories deemphasize the losses relative to the wins. For them, losses are more like near wins, so they expect that their luck will even out in the future, and their true skill will prevail. In general we can say that our memories (via hind sight bias) are kind to our past behavior, and spur us on to continue what we're doing rather than change.

If our beliefs are old and not used much, they may have outlasted the original rationale, if there ever was one. If we've forgotten our original justification, we're left with just the feeling for or against the belief. It might be wrong, but unless System 2 is highly motivated to revisit the justification, the status quo lives to fight another day. If System 2 is comfortable (that is, in a state of cognitive ease), there may not be much motivation to do this work. Not enough motivation, no change.

Our emphasis on the usefulness of the memories of eyewitnesses in jury trials turns out to be less reliable than you might expect. The Innocence Project has overturned some 300 cases of guilt of which some 75% were due in large part to faulty eye-witness. Nearly a third of all overturned cases were due to more than one eyewitness. There are many factors that could promote these kinds of errors, and one of these is the likelihood that since we are biased to believe, we are also more likely than not to believe the selected suspect is actually the perpetrator. With all of this and more working against the dependability of our memories, it is no wonder that Sir William Blackstone in the 1700's wrote: "All presumptive evidence of felony should be admitted cautiously: for the law holds, that it is better that ten guilty people escape, that one innocent suffer." [188]

Pride and Prejudice

Pride certainly is a factor for why we are **prejudiced** against change. If we are not the owner of the new idea, and if we don't get on board with it early, we don't like to look like we were late for the dance. He who laughs last didn't 'get it. "It is more often from pride than from ignorance that we are so obstinately opposed to current opinions; we find the first places taken, and we do not want to be the last."—Francois De La Rochefoucauld moralist (1613-1680)

"A compounding problem is that to the extent that a sense of pride arises out of feelings of uniqueness or originality, we are divided in our motivation. We want to be known for having original ideas, inspired hunches, and gut feelings that make a difference. Indeed, a "well-honed sixth sense" is considered a measure of the good clinician. But being a good doctor also requires sticking with the best medical evidence, even if it contradicts your personal experience. We need to distinguish between gut feeling and testable knowledge, between hunches and empirically tested evidence."[189]

Another reason not to change when it appears advisable to do so is that some will think it makes them look smarter if they don't flip flop. We may look foolish and project a lack of authority or expertness when we do so. We don't like

---

[188] Baron pg 233
[189] Burton pg 161

to admit that our beliefs may be wrong, and flip flopping contains that admission. Let the facts fall where they may, we need to keep up appearances. Credibility is more easily lost than recovered.

Appearing uncertain can give the impression that we are short on expertise.[190] Even open mindedness could be detrimental to the appearance and maintenance of expertise. To avoid this, we latch on to a belief and don't entertain doubt.[191]

"Another possibility is that people confuse two different standards for thinking, which we might call the 'good thinker' (active open-mindedness) and the expert. Because experts know the answer to most questions, they usually do not have to consider alternatives or counterevidence. If we admire experts, we may come to admire people who are "decisive" in the sense of being rigid. When a news commentator criticizes a political candidate for waffling and being unsure (as might befit a good thinker faced with many of the complex issues that politicians must face), the implication is that the candidate is not expert enough to have figured out the right answer. Similarly, a person who adopts a know-it-all tone—speaking without qualification or doubt—is giving a sign of expertise. Some parents (perhaps because they are experts about the matter under discussion) talk this way to their children, who come to think of it as a 'grown-up' way to talk."[192]

---

[190]   "He who asks is a fool for five minutes, but he who does not ask remains a fool forever." Chinese Proverb

[191]   "Faith which does not doubt is dead faith." Miguel de Unamuno, philosopher and writer (1864-1936)

[192]   Baron pg 214

Reliance on experts-halo effect

As Shermer writes, we want, we are biased, to believe. This can lead us into gullibility, and gullibility is associated with feelings of overconfidence (I don't need to verify, I trust this journalist). We may have good reason to be trusting (more so in older people, due to a drop in anterior insular activity, SA MIND May/June 2013, also Fine pg 9), but we tend to over extend the feeling to believe that the trusted source is also to be believed in areas outside her expertise. We fit new information into our ongoing story of this person we trust, as long as it is not inconsistent with what we already think. This is the Halo Effect where, in our urge to simplify and categorize, we think that if, for example, in our judgment of this presidential candidate got it right on environmental issues, she's probably spot on in other areas such as tax reform. With no other information, there is no basis for this kind of thinking to extend trust just to be consistent. As our belief grows for this hallowed and haloed one, we accept more readily anything she does. Unless proven otherwise, this trust will solidify, and along with it, our resistance to change.

If we don't like something, for instance, the technology that extracts gas from shale, we will carry that over to the possible benefits of this technology and its inverse relation with its risks. We will see fewer redeeming values than if we liked the technology. We link low benefits with high risk. Good benefits with low risk. This feels good because we like consistency. We will have to fight this urge for coherence, for certainty, in order to react objectively to the evidence. In the end, it's a lot of work to change, to live with ambiguity.

Anchor Heuristic

As its name suggests, another guide that works against change is the Anchor Heuristic (AH). When we are exposed to a value prior to estimating an unrelated number, the AH takes the value into consideration in order to influence the estimate. In situations where this occurs, we are artificially limited in our subsequent estimation of a quantity. We are tethered to the anchor and allowed to adjust, but only by just so much. Usually this adjustment doesn't quite make it to the true value.

As Lehrer explained it[193], "In essence, the anchoring effect is about the brain's spectacular inability to dismiss irrelevant information. The problem is that the rational brain isn't good at disregarding facts, even when it knows those facts are useless."

Kahneman, pg 483 of Nobel Prize: "Most behavior is intuitive, skilled, unproblematic and successful (Klein 1998). In some fraction of cases, a need to correct the intuitive judgments and preferences will be acknowledged, but the intuitive impression will be the anchor of the judgment. Under-correction is more likely than over—correction in such cases."

The implications of forming anchors that are hard to change imply that we are less able to see another side of an argument, less able to empathize, less able to take another's perspective. If we first get a positive assessment of one side of an argument, it acts like an anchor and makes it more difficult to change to the other side of the argument. On the other hand, having less empathy helps compensate for our poor sense of deception detection.

We are also anchored by first impressions which tend to become lasting impressions. Anchors as beliefs are easier to drop than to hoist, so the effect of the anchor is that we

---

[193]   Lehrer pg 157

may linger longer before changing our beliefs. Additional experiences with the same person, product, or experience may not overcome the effects of the anchor. Initial encounters count. Stability, or coherence over time, is a comforting thought, and the comfort of keeping the status quo is compelling.

The flexibility of an anchor can be affected by its precision. High precision gives the impression that much is known about the number. If this is not true we will be fooled into believing the value carries more information than it does. Confidence in this piece of the story would consequently be solidified. Conversely, a number with low precision will not garner the same trust in its truth as it would generate if it were more precise. Low precision does, however, allow greater flexibility in making the story cohesive and coherent. Herbert pg 123. "It turns out that a precise anchor is also a stronger anchor—people are more uncomfortable straying from a precise anchor than a round one."

The other day I was renting a car and the person handling my case told me he had to leave and would be back in 4 minutes. I took that to mean probably less the 6 minutes. His use of the high precision 4 instead of 'about 5' surprised me, so my mind made up a story that he's done this short task so many times he was very sure how long it would take. His precision was probably meant to instill confidence in me that he would be back very shortly. He returned over ten minutes later than the original estimate. Being gullible, I had made my anchor his precise 4 minutes. I felt I had been manipulated by the use of precision. In my short stay in his office I heard this kind of unjustifiably high precision a couple of times. Had he been taught to take advantage of this power of the Anchoring Heuristic? "There is nothing worse than a sharp [precise] image of a fuzzy concept." Ansel Adams

Since an intuitive idea first comes from the unconscious, it can serve as an anchor for the System 2 adjustment[194]. This being true, the anchor should be quite lasting, and since we're not aware of the source of this anchoring heuristic, it's very hard to change. The rash trumps the rational.

Your physical state of being can also influence your susceptibility to the anchoring effect. System 2 will adjust less from an anchor when you are well rested and nourished.[195] Again, it's harder to change when the source of the belief to be changed is not available to our conscious.

"For the ordinary business of life an ounce of habit is worth a pound of intellect." Thomas B. Reed

It's a slippery slope down to the habitat of habit, an uphill climb to escape it.

While habit does have its upside (I almost always put my keys in the same place, so since my first option when looking for them is often right, I don't usually waste time by starting with second options) it does have the downside of lazily dismissing out of hand, options that deserve consideration. This is especially true if there is a change in the environment relevant to the validity of the process, to the design space, if you will. In a controlled, stable environment, for a task that you repeat frequently and get immediate feedback, once you have established a routine that gives predictable results, committing it to habit frees up some thinking space. Habit: don't think of it is so much of as being a crutch[196] as of its being a wheel chair. The essence of habit is to be able to repeat the same actions without thinking about them. Because we don't think about

---

[194] Kahneman's nobel, pg 473

[195] K2011 pg 43/4

[196] "Habit with him was all the test of truth, / It must be right: I've done it from my youth." -George Crabbe, poet and naturalist

them, we eventually become unaware of them, and they become difficult to change because we don't even know we have them. They also serve to cement the feeling that what you are doing by habit is supported by some long forgotten truth that the habit reflects. First we make our habits, then our habits make us.

Affect Heuristic (AH): Reliance on intuitions/emotions . . . 2nd thoughts

"The [unconscious] heart has arguments with which the logic of the [conscious] mind is not acquainted." Blaise Pascal

What is the AH? The essential concept of the AH is that our emotions play a role in the decision making process. This role often preempts the deliberative thought process.

How does the Affect Heuristic make it difficult to change our beliefs? It is often argued that a balanced input of emotions and rational thinking is necessary for good decision making and risk taking. Where there are no emotions, due for example to brain damage in areas such as the amygdala, we get a situation of analysis paralysis. Without emotions we struggle with even the simplest of decisions. If we, like Buridan's ass, can't make a decision between the equidistant food bucket and the water bucket, we don't change, we don't choose either in time to avoid problems or in time to not miss opportunities.

Fear is a much studied emotion and is intimately linked to the stress of decision making. This is especially true when not all the necessary information is available. Under these ambiguous conditions[197] we can relieve this uncertainty by

---

[197]   SA Mind May/June 2013 "Uncertainty appears to affect people by sapping the same kind of attention resources required to exert self-control."

making a decision, good or bad. The Affect Heuristic eases
this stress by changing the question to an easier one that
relies on emotions. Asked 'which is better', we answer the
easier 'which do I like more'. Resolution of the ambiguity,
of the uncertainty that spurs this stress, makes us feel
better.[198] However, some decisions can leave us wondering
what would be the effects of our answers if they turn out to
be wrong. Will the possibility of regret lead us to inaction,
not making a decision?

While the AH can reduce the fear factor when different
options are available for a decision, the thought of regret
is an emotion that travels along with the fear of making
an error in judgment. We dread making mistakes, because
we dread the regret that accompanies our errors. This
being the case, we plan our decisions, taking into account
different outcomes and how we might feel depending upon
the results. Emotions, products of the S1, can affect your
decisions, and the outcomes of your decisions can affect
your emotions. One possible common denominator in
this vicious loop is regret. You fear a decision will lead to
regret and when it does, regret feeds your fear of the same
happening in the future. You anticipate the outcomes of
your decision, and you don't want to be wrong, for regret
will be yours.

Here are a couple of studies related to these points.

Results of the following experiment, show that fear
of regret can bias our choice between high and low risk
gambles.

> There is a risky gamble and a safe gamble, tested
> to be about equally attractive. If you think you
> will learn only the results of the risky gamble and
> not learn the results of the safe, you don't worry

---

[198] Desalvo pg 32 "Our need to be right is actually a need to 'feel'
right."

so much about feelings of regret, so you're free to choose the risky gamble. Under this condition 61 per cent chose the risky gamble. If you expect to learn the results of the safe gamble, you are less likely to chose the risky gamble (only 23 per cent did), because if you lose, you may have to face the fact that the safe gamble might have been a better choice, causing you the emotion of regret. Now, regret is not all bad, and in fact provides feedback for the learning process. Other emotions also have a role in helping us evaluate our experiences. The power of negative thinking. The possibility of regret prods us to more thoroughly evaluate our options.

In another study,

> subjects read a short report extolling either the wonderful benefits or the low level of risks associated with a technology. Where the report spoke only to benefits, subject's perception of risk also decreased to become aligned more positively with those opinions. The same alignment occurred when the report indicated risks were high (so benefits were judged to be lower). Apparently the need for consistency won over the need to be objective. Here we see that liking something based on benefits also leads to minimizing the impact of risks.

We can more easily make decisions when there is no contradictory information. When there is, for example in risk/benefit analyses, we can remove the contradictory information by aligning higher risk with lower benefits or higher benefits with lower risks. We make the contradiction disappear, but at what cost?

The emotional effects of outcomes both good and bad should be taken into account. If one state of nature is much different than another, the regret will also be large. Should the state be 'dry' then the difference in outcomes for choosing to carry or not to carry an umbrella is small, and as a result, not very emotional. If the state is rain, then the difference in the two outcomes for choosing to carry or not an umbrella, are larger that when the state is dry. Emotions as part of the outcome of our decisions must be considered should our model of the state of nature be correct or not. Understanding the level of risk and consequent emotional cost depending on the assumed difference between states of nature is advised.[199]

One way to reduce the occurrence of regret is to decline the choice that would lead to greater responsibility. We respond to the problem by advocating either change or no change. Since a greater sense of responsibility is generally associated with the former, we tend to stay with the status quo. We don't change.

We easily learn to associate noxious situations with fear. Many of these learning associations are likely to last for life, they're that important. I can remember as a child getting sick after eating some canned ravioli. I was quite surprised when years later, just the site of a can of ravioli brought back some of that same visceral nausea. These memories and associated reactions are hard to change, and with good reason. We may not be able to afford another exposure to this 'food'. These memories are keepers.

Much of our decision making behavior is explained as seeking the goal of being at cognitive ease. Beliefs become engrained in our behavior when their use shows some consistency in arriving and staying in this happy state of being. If the patterns we discover are good at predicting

---

[199]   Baron pg 275

results, over time their continued success is valued, and they become trusted, reliable beliefs, earning a deserved tenure.

I see this tenure phase as the mental hardwiring that we are born with, programmed to develop in ways that promoted survival in another time and place. We are wired to win. This is the DNA where our ancestors' beliefs, truths, and memories are housed. Our behavior reflects their winning performance. We hang our unique, personal learning on this scaffold we're born with. When applied in the wrong current context, our actions lead us to ask ourselves, What Were We Thinking? Changing or replacing inappropriate behavior can be a formidable task, even when justified.

Consider how we fortify memories. Our memories and beliefs over time are exposed to ever more evidence (as accumulation of confirmatory evidence continues to occur), however false, that solidify our beliefs as truths. As the years pass by, it takes more effort just to keep on keeping on, with little energy left to deal with change. This reserve is limited and not easily recharged. Little wonder it's a rare treat to find minds open to change among the age-challenged.

Our natural tendency is to look for and remember evidence that supports our beliefs. The discomfort from the dissonance of contradictory information is not easily accommodated[200] so as Bacon wrote, (see above) we devalue

---

[200] "In The Crack-up, F.Scott Fitzgerald wrote . . . 'The test of a first-rate intelligence is the ability to hold two opposed ideas in the mind at the same time and still retain the ability to function.'"

Shermer pg 135 speaks of ". . . our natural tendency to accept as true that which we can comprehend quickly." This is consistent with experiments where true statements were identified as such quicker than false statements were. (pg 133/4). Painting with a very broad brush, we are lazily and naturally gullible, not scientifically skeptical. This is also

or totally dump the information that challenges our beliefs. Why? Because this makes for a cleaner, less ambiguous belief. Why clutter it with exceptions and incongruent details?

The blind faith of ignorant confidence

Here are a few thoughts on the problem of why the unskilled are so overconfident, from which follows a lack of perceived need to change.

Those that are under skilled are often not skilled enough to know how relatively little they know nor how much they don't know, so they overate themselves. For the skilled, there is greater awareness that much of their skills could be improved, and so they underrate themselves. "Thus, the miscalibration of the incompetent stems from an error about the self, whereas the miscalibration of the highly competent stems from an error about others." This is the Dunning-Kruger effect[201]—a twofold bias. On one hand the lack of skills robs them of the ability to realize their errors, leading to the delusion of the incompetent

---

consistent with Spinoza's idea that we have to first understand a concept enough to believe it before the process of disbelieving becomes possible. Disbelieving takes an extra step, and this is why it's relatively a lot of work. In order to disbelieve, we have to behold the belief before we can unbelieve or reject it. It is particularly difficult when we try to disbelieve our own thoughts and model of the world. Access to our own arguments for our ideas is much easier than looking for information to the contrary.

[201] Kruger, Justin; David Dunning (1999). "Unskilled and Unaware of It: How Difficulties in Recognizing One's Own Incompetence Lead to Inflated Self-Assessments". *Journal of Personality and Social Psychology* **77** (6): 1121-34. doi:10.1037/0022-3514.77.6.1121. PMID 10626367. http://citeseerx.ist.psu.edu/viewdoc/download?doi=10.1.1.64.2655&rep=rep1&type=pdf.

to overrate their own capabilities. Part of the reason for this overconfidence may lie in the lack of skill which may interfere with the ability to recognize skill in others or in their own shortcomings. On the other hand, skilled people underrate their abilities, as they assume others have a similar understanding. This is called the false consensus effect. "The skills that enable one to construct a grammatical sentence are the skills necessary to recognize a grammatical sentence, and thus are the same skills necessary to determine if a grammatical mistake has been made. In short, the same knowledge that underlies the ability to produce correct judgment is also the knowledge that underlies the ability to recognize correct judgment. To lack the former is to be deficient in the latter."[202] While one might expect the skilled to offer constructive criticism, depending on the situation, it may never seem to be the socially right moment to do so. ('If you don't have something nice to say, keep it to yourself.') This being the case, lack of feedback could add to the continued incompetence.

"Our reluctance to face the problems of the rational mind stems in part from the feeling that the mind isn't of the same category as the body. We don't expect to jump twenty feet high or to swim underwater for a week; we can easily feel our physical limitations. But we don't feel the same limits on our thoughts. For example, you feel free to accept or reject this paragraph. Acknowledging all the subliminal factors that influence this decision doesn't override the more powerful feeling that you are in control

---

[202] To be ignorant of one's ignorance is the malady of the ignorant. Amos B. Alcott,

Not ignorance, but ignorance of ignorance, is the death of knowledge. -Alfred North Whitehead, mathematician and philosopher (1861-1947).

of your thoughts. Our mental limitations prevent us from accepting our mental limitations."[203]

A few thoughts on this theme of knowledge and doubt:

"Ignorance more frequently begets confidence than does knowledge." Charles Darwin

"The trouble with the world is that the stupid are cocksure and the intelligent full of doubt." Bertrand Russell

"We know accurately only when we know little, with knowledge doubt increases." Johann Wolfgang Von Goethe

David Gross, the 2004 recipient of the Nobel Prize in physics, said, "The most important product of knowledge is ignorance."[204] This is consistent with the teaching that good science creates more questions than it answers.

By the way, those of you who think you know everything are annoying to those of us who do.

First impressions

Blink pg 36 On a related situation where information was limited, Gladwell wrote: "What this suggests is that it is quite possible for people who have never met us and who have spent only twenty minutes thinking about us to come to a better understanding of who we are than people who have known us for years." First impressions are probably more reliable than we suspect, and that's why it's been evolutionarily advantageous to make them stick. Rapid and accurate judgments are an efficient use of time.

In the article "The Confidence of Eyewitnesses in Their Identifications From Lineups, Vol. 2, Number 5, October 2002, Current Directions in Psychological Sciences, Wells et. al. wrote "Studies have consistently demonstrated that the confidence an eyewitness expresses in an identification

---

[203] Burton pg 159
[204] Burton pg 224

is the major factor determining whether people will believe that the eyewitness made an accurate identification." In the Federally mandated Innocence Project, eyewitnesses consistently demonstrated high confidence in cases that were later overturned. It would seem reasonable to think that the more time an eye witness spends looking at a suspect, the greater the confidence in his judgment will be. However, "Eyewitnesses who make their identification decision quickly (in 10 seconds or less) are considerably more likely to be accurate than are eyewitnesses who take longer."

Our confidence in our beliefs, and all the related support for that confidence, acts to keep things as they are.

Back to the future: predictions and the feeling of control

As we continue learning, we arrive at the level of being able to predict. Being good at predicting translates into the ability to control, and that is a satisfying feeling, the feeling of cognitive ease that we earlier identified as one of the goals that justifies, and is a measure of, how effective our beliefs and decisions are. One way to achieve greater predictability is to actually create the future we want. As an example, you could move into a gated community to reduce the uncertainty of being a victim of criminality. The good feeling we derive from the sense of being able to control contrasts with the stress from lack of control. While we might not actually be in control, the important thing (as far as cognitive ease goes) is that we *feel* that we are in control.

A common companion with feeling in control is the illusion of being able to assign a pattern to a random process. When flipping a coin gives heads five times in a row, we bet on tails, thinking it's due. According to our thinking, we've found a pattern in this random process. If this feels good, mission accomplished. Order is restored.

This 'pattern' gets us out of the uncomfortable feeling of ambiguity. It's just a little self-delusion, but it effectively combats uncertainty. Tails I win, heads are out of my control. This is called the Attribution Bias. Wins are due to my being above average.

One of the difficulties in the process of change is that the idea or belief that now deserves changing was originally formed by our unconscious mind. Since by definition we are unconscious of it (S1) and so unconscious of its influence on our decisions, we become like Swift's man who can't be changed by reason, because reason wasn't the cause of his belief in the first place. Let's follow this idea and parse out the inputs to this unconscious belief.

"The Schultz experiments followed a simple protocol: he sounded a loud tone, waited for a few seconds, and then squirted some drops of apple juice into the mouth of a monkey. While the experiment was unfolding, Schultz was probing the monkey brain with a needle that monitored the electrical activity inside individual cells. At first, the dopamine neurons fired only when the juice was delivered. The cells were responding to the actual reward. However, once the animal learned that the tone preceded the arrival of juice—this required only a few trials—the same neurons began firing at the sound of the tone instead of at the sweet reward. Schultz called these cells "prediction neurons," since they were more concerned with predicting rewards than actually receiving them . . . Once this simple pattern was learned, the monkeys' dopamine neurons became exquisitely sensitive to variations on it. If the cellular predictions proved correct, and the reward arrived right on time, then the primate experienced a brief surge of dopamine, the pleasure of being right. However, if the pattern was violated-if the tone was played but the juice never arrived—then the monkey's dopamine neurons decreased their firing rate. This is known as the prediction—error signal. The monkey felt 'upset' because its prediction of getting a drink was wrong."[205] Adjustments on a synaptic level, deep change, isn't easy.

Why on earth do we predict so much? The practice of predicting is like experimentation, in that it is a pathway to learning. Failure or success, we learn from the practice of predicting. If results are surprising, all the better as they may push us to revamp our beliefs, our inadequate models of how things work. What we need to be careful of and control for is randomness. Prediction depends on pattern formation, and we are so good at creating patterns even when there are none, our predictions may inexplicably fall short of being correct.

To sum up, the power to predict or illusion of same leads to cognitive ease. When this ability breaks down, our disappointment is reflected in a neurotransmitter imbalance.

Too Much Information

"Finally, in another telling experiment, the psychologist Paul Slovic asked bookmakers to select from eight variables in past horse races those that they found useful in computing the odds. These variables included all manner of statistical information about past performances. The bookmakers were given the ten most useful variables, then asked to predict the outcome of races. Then they were given ten more and asked to predict again. The increase in the information set did not lead to an increase in their accuracy; their confidence in their choices, on the other hand, went up markedly. Information proved to be toxic."[206]

When **cognitive dissonance**, defined here as a perceived gap between our beliefs and information to the contrary, is present, there is a need to reduce this unpleasant condition

---

[205] Lehrer pg 36
[206] Taleb black pg 145

of cognitive stress. We bridge this gap by updating our beliefs or by defending them. Defending (maintaining the status quo belief) requires less thought, less energy, than taking the initiative and time to challenge the current state, and so defending against change is usually the dominant choice. There is less time and perhaps credibility, with a new idea, so changing to it requires extra effort. It is less likely to win over older, more familiar ideas.

This practice of defense of a prior belief is sometimes referred to as the Experimenter's or Expectation bias—the tendency for experimenters to believe and publish data that agree with their expectations[207] for the outcome of an experiment, and to disbelieve, discard, or downgrade the corresponding weightings for data that appear to conflict with those expectations.[208] The tendency is to search for or interpret information in a way that confirms one's preconceptions. We want to believe that we are objective, but to some extent we are influenced by the heuristic known as the Bias Blind Spot—a common error of viewing oneself as not vulnerable to bias.

"Belief which leaves no place for doubt is not a belief; it is a superstition." Jose Bergamin, author (1895-1983)

It takes trust to have the faith to delegate decision making. This faith is sometimes ill-founded, but is nevertheless comforting. The roots of closed mindedness are sometimes institutional, that is, we are overconfident

---

[207] See Harvard Professor's story earlier in this chapter.

[208] The Queen remarked," . . . Now I'll give you something to believe. I'm just one hundred and one, five months and a day." "I can't believe that!" said Alice. "Can't you?" the Queen said in a pitying tone. "Try again: draw a long breath, and shut your eyes." Alice laughed. "There's no use trying," she said, "one can't believe impossible things." "I daresay you haven't had much practice," said the Queen. "When I was your age, I always did it for half-an-hour a day. Why, sometimes I've believed as many as six impossible things before breakfast."

in those institutions with whom we have delegated responsibility for making decisions. The survival of organizations with which we associate some of our beliefs may depend on its members' unchanging beliefs[209] in the institution's unyielding principles. We may feel linked to an authority or institution to which we have essentially delegated responsibility for a judgment. If they don't change, we don't change. Who do we trust? A skeptical message on a sign in an Amherst College laboratory: "In God we trust, the rest must bring data." Jesus saith unto him, Thomas, because thou hast seen me, thou hast believed: blessed are they that have *not* seen, and *yet* have believed. The less you know, the more you may believe.

Being close minded is a comfortable[210] place to be, and since inquiry is fatal to certainty[211], inquiry is neither

---

[209] Baron pg 214 "To keep its adherents from one generation to the next, each of these institutions must convince them that its views are correct, even though many outsiders will argue otherwise. Those institutions that inculcate an ideology in which defense of one's belief is a virtue and questioning is a vice are the ones most likely to overcome challenges from outside." If ownership of a decision has been delegated to the institution, and I have faith in and trust my institution's decision, I will not change.

[210] "Doubt is *not* a pleasant condition, but certainty is an absurd one." Voltaire. This assertion that doubt is not a pleasant condition was studied by Ming Hsu et al., in "Neural Systems Responding to Degrees of Uncertainty in Human Decision—making," Science 310 (December 2005): 1680-83. They found that even small amounts of ambiguity increased activity in the amygdala, the site considered to be the fear center of the brain. The resolution of this ambiguity sometimes requires that a decision be made. In turn, being faced with having to make a decision is often accompanied by the fear of regret, the fear of making the wrong decision. Faced with all these sources of fear, we look to simplify reality in order to facilitate achievement of cognitive ease.

[211] Will Durant, historian (1885-1981)

comforting nor actively pursued by the closed minded. With more knowledge comes more doubt. Inquiry may leave us with more questions than answers, opening up a can of new problems that we would rather not. Closed minds are antithetical to the pursuit of change.

The educational system

Education is what survives when what has been learnt has been forgotten. B.F. Skinner

As Burton wrote, "I cannot help wondering if an educational system that promotes black or white and yes or no answers might be affecting how reward systems develop in our youth. If the fundamental thrust of education is "being correct" rather than acquiring a thoughtful awareness of ambiguities, inconsistencies, and underlying paradoxes, it is easy to see how the reward systems might be molded to prefer certainty over open-mindedness.[212] To the extent that doubt is less emphasized, there will be far more risk in asking tough questions. Conversely, we, like rats rewarded for pressing the bar, will stick with the tried-and-true responses."[213] Under these conditions, we are less likely to question and we are more likely to avoid nuances. We stick with our simple, ideal model of the world.

We are generally so opposed to change that even when we do change, we cover our tracks. Kahnemann said[214] in an interview, "I mean, the thing that is absolutely the most striking is how seldom people change their minds. First, we're not aware of changing our minds even when we do change our minds. And most people, after they change

---

[212] Just think of the tragedy of teaching children not to doubt. -Clarence Darrow, lawyer and author (1857-1938)

[213] Burton pg 99

[214] Hallinan pg 59

their minds, reconstruct their past opinion—they believe they always thought that." This Hind Sight bias is the name given to the thinking that I knew it all the time, the results were inevitable.

"In a less regular, or low-validity, environment, the heuristics of judgment are invoked. System 1 is often able to produce quick answers to difficult questions by substitution, creating coherence where this is none." "This is why subjective confidence is not a good diagnostic of accuracy: judgments that answer the wrong question (type 3 error) can also be made with high confidence." [215]

K2011 pg 239 "Earlier I traced people's confidence in a belief of two related impressions: cognitive ease and coherence. We feel confident when the story we tell ourselves comes easily to mind, with no contradiction and no competing scenario. But ease and coherence do not guarantee that a belief held with confidence is true. The associative machine is sct to suppress doubt and to evoke ideas and information that are compatible with the currently dominant story. A mind that follows WYSIATI will achieve high confidence much too easily by ignoring what it does not know." And we have seen how high confidence relates to change.

As Bob Dylan sang about change, "he not busy being born is busy dying".

---

[215] K2011 pg 243

Chapter 5

SUMMERTIME, AND THE
LIVING IS EASY.

STORIES

The universe is not made of atoms, but of stories. Muriel Rukeyser
"Ideas come and go, stories stay"[216]

"We're storytelling creatures by nature, and we tell
ourselves story after story[217] until we come up with an

---

[216] Taleb Black prologue xxxi

[217] The comedic TV series Get Smart had a running joke that
Maxwell would try to convince someone of an extreme claim
or situation that the person being spoken to finds incredulous.
Max then follows up with a couple of, "would you believe . . . ?"
to get to the opposite extreme.

Badeff: You like that, Mr. Wilcox? Are you certain you're a
music lover?

Maxwell Smart: Well, of course I am. Why, do you know that

explanation that we like and that sounds reasonable
enough to believe. And when the story portrays us in a
more glowing and positive light, so much the better."
Ariely pg 165

"We have, as human beings, a storytelling problem.
We're a bit too quick to come up with explanations for
things we don't really have an explanation for."[218]

For our purposes, stories provide us with information that
can impact our decision making. One way in which a story
can have a positive impact is by simplifying information.
This produces a calming effect so that we can be at ease
and think more clearly. Good stories entertain us, and
that entertainment value is measured as a degree of CE
(cognitive ease). CE, for its part, is that state of mind that is
calm and unworried, unhurried. Physical needs are under
control and the feeling of familiarity feeds confidence
and security, and that breeds content. On the other hand,
stories that seem inconsistent result in a state of cognitive
stress. These fixer uppers sometimes require thinking that
uses the Halo effect, myside bias, and whatever else that
may serve to smooth and lay the stress to rest.

The following will build on much of what we have
discussed in previous chapters in relation to heuristics and
biases. We will see how System 1 continually spins stories in
which correlated ideas and concepts are brought together
quickly with whatever information is available. Heuristics,

I once listened to 3 straight weeks of Beethoven? Would you
believe it? 3 weeks of Beethoven!
Badeff: I find that hard to believe.
Maxwell Smart: Would you believe 2 weeks of Bach?
Badeff: I don't think so.
Maxwell Smart: How about an hour of Looney Tunes?
[218]   Blinkpg69, Malcolm Gladwell, Blink: The Power of Thinking
Without Thinking, 2005

with all their baggage, are deployed in this process to simplify concepts and bridge knowledge gaps. System 2, time permitting, can put these stories to the test. We will look at how these tests favor a certain class of explanations over others, and how they have been a part of the evolution of learning and belief formation.

Stories[219] work to achieve CE in part by simplifying and summarizing so as to overpower those rivals of CE; dissonance, uncertainty, and ambiguity. Effective stories need neither be true nor complete. Another worrisome outcome of our reliance on stories is summarized by Taleb as the 'narrative fallacy' which ". . . addresses our limited ability to look at sequences of facts without weaving an explanation into them, or, equivalently, forcing a logical link, an arrow of relationship, upon them. Explanations bind facts together. Stories make information all the more easily remembered; they help them make more sense. Where this propensity can go wrong is when it increases our impression of understanding."[220] Not understanding, but the *impression* of understanding. In this fallacy, we classify and create patterns that reduce uncertainty by substituting rules and categories for what is often unrecognized randomness. The devil is in the messy details, details made invisible by having been swept into simplified silos. This process makes stories more convincing by making

---

[219] For our purposes, the word 'story' will include explanations and other devices such as experimental results, patternicity, assumptions, hypotheses, and in general, models of how the world works to support congruence, cohesiveness, and coherence. Here, what I call a 'story' or 'narrative' might be better thought of as a vignette, in that we will be dealing with very short scenes or descriptions. Nevertheless, this is my narrative and I'm sticking with it so this is the last time you will hear the 'v' word.

[220] Taleb Black pg.63-4

the situation appear less nuanced than it really is. We innocently think we know what we do not know.[221]

Taleb wrote[222] "We . . . have a hunger for rules because we need to reduce the dimension of matters so they can get into our heads. Or, rather, sadly, so we can squeeze them into our heads. The more random information is, the greater the dimensionality, and thus the more difficult to summarize. The more you summarize, the more order you put in, the less randomness. Hence the same condition that makes us simplify pushes us to think that the world is less random than it actually is."

The individual and the statistic

One death is a tragedy; a million is a statistic. Stalin

We are built to understand the individual narrative. As Paulos noted,[223] "In listening to stories we are inclined to suspend disbelief so as to be entertained, whereas in evaluating statistics we are inclined to suspend belief so as not to be beguiled." Two things. Stories are generally entertaining, pleasurable, relatable, while the purpose of statistical evaluation is to ". . . not to be beguiled." We drop our defenses and allow ourselves to believe and enjoy a good story while our rational mind fears being fooled, a generally less pleasurable feeling. Is it any wonder that we are prone to elevate and apply the individual narrative to infer our model of the world, while the statistical job of going in the other direction and deducing the individual

---

[221]   K2011pg201 "Paradoxically, it is easier to construct a coherent story when you know little, when there are fewer pieces to fit into the puzzle. Our comforting conviction that the world makes sense rests on a secure foundation: our almost unlimited ability to ignore our ignorance."

[222]   Taleb Black pg 69

[223]   Paulos pg 32

from the model is less easily accomplished?[224] As well, this
'not to be beguiled' requires addressing the concept of
absence, which is not a strong suit of our environmental
monitor, S1. S1 only works with what's there, not what's not.
Kahneman expressed this as S1 "WYSIATI" (what you see
is all there is). Statistics should fulfill the role of including
'what's not there' in its analyses. Statistical abstractions such
as 'average' or 'standard deviation' are not what our senses
detect but rather tools that our rational mind tries to use to
make objective evaluations.[225] This statistical story can be, as
we saw with the Challenger data, surprisingly subject to the
subjective mind where intuitions may sway the day.

If it's all we have, we weave our model of the world from
the individual story. The degree to which this individual
story is salient, recent, and available[226] to our memories
can bias the degree of belief we have in its frequency and
probability of being representative of our models, our
expectations of the world. That the degree of belief can
be biased is witnessed by the example of how our estimates
of the frequency of car accidents increase right after we
witness one. Our confidence in the representativeness
of the individual to the whole is legendarily prone to

---

[224] A very cool word related to substituting the individual for the
general and vice versa:

syn·ec·do·che :

A figure of speech in which a part is used for the
whole (as *hand* for *sailor*), the whole for a part
(as *the law* for *police officer*), the specific for the
general (as *cutthroat* for *assassin*), the general for
the specific (as *thief* for *pickpocket*), or the material
for the thing made from it (as *steel* for *sword*).

[225] Taleb Black pg 121 "Out of sight, out of mind: we harbor a
natural, even physical, scorn of the abstract."

[226] When the narrative is more available, it is also judged as more
likely, truer.

gullibility. This is due in large part to our neglect of the role of random variation.[227] We order a meal at a restaurant for the first time, and it comes out cold. Our model of the quality of the whole restaurant will be negative, unless our friends tell us we were just unlucky. Or were they just lucky . . . ?

Imagine the following comes on the TV. We see a woman open a refrigerator and pull out three small rations of food that she had prepared, one for her and one each for her two young children, Josh and Joanna. Their mom is working two jobs but it's not enough. The future looks bleak. The children are seen going to bed hungry with medical conditions they can't afford to be treated for. The family is suffering economically and on the edge of living on the streets.

During the elections of 2008 and ensuing years of debate on the affordable health care act, politicians were quick to see that giving concrete examples of the predicament of individual families was an effective way of illustrating how ineffective the current health care system was at providing care for those who really need it. Although this story is anecdotal, it probably impacts you more by evoking more sympathetic emotion than would a statistical rundown of say, the increased number of families that were buying medicines off the Internet from unknown providers just because they are more affordable[228]. Health care policy makers understand this and accordingly choose stories of individuals to make their points. We are easily misled by such stories into believing that they are representative of a larger whole. Our feelings are sensitive to our senses (S1), and what we sense is palpable and more easily imagined

---

[227] We want closure and we're uncomfortable when the explanation is that the results are due to random variation.

[228] Facts are stubborn, but statistics are more pliable. Mark Twain

and remembered, than, for example, the statistical abstraction we call the pie chart. Poverty has a face.

System 2, on the other hand, is able to take advantage of a larger view of the possibilities. It can incorporate information on averages and characterizations of populations into the task of rationalizing its decisions. It can take into account what is not happening. Nevertheless, it will unlikely be more persuasive than an emotionally driven decision.

One of the themes of this book is that statistical thinking does not come naturally. Recall Kahneman's Nobel prize Lecture, where he said: "Our first joint article examined *systematic errors* in the casual statistical judgments of statistically sophisticated researchers. Remarkably, the intuitive judgments of these experts did not conform to statistical principles with which they were thoroughly familiar . . . . we were impressed by the persistence of discrepancies between statistical intuition and statistical knowledge . . ." How does this relate to storytelling? Here we should remember what we do when a question or the search for missing information is too difficult. We use heuristics and often change the question. This substitution is designed to help make a decision in order to make us feel good and succeeds to the extent that it appears to resolve dissonance or incompleteness of the situation. Most of the time this change of question is innocuous, no harm is done. The resulting biased decision diverts the storyline down a path where we feel confident in the analysis of the situation, the story. However, this confidence in a story is built on misdirection and oversimplification

System 1 thinks in terms of individual stories more than statistical aggregations or group characteristics. System 2 is charged with not ". . . mistaking anecdotes for statistical evidence or, conversely, taking averages to be descriptive of individual cases."[229]

---

[229]   Paulos pg 5 The plural of anecdote is not data.

The strengths of stories are often double edged. The same characteristics that make them attractive also tend to make them biased, misleading. Stories are attractive in that they simplify and unify in order to help make a situation more understandable and memorable. Unfortunately this mental economy is often achieved by a concurrent abandonment of information.[230] This is not necessarily a bad thing. We will see how at times reduced information can produce a leaner decision making environment with less chatter, less restrictions, greater speed and accuracy. This seems to fly in the face of common wisdom that tells us more information is better. [231] At times when your intuition is working well, you're having a good day hitting golf balls or knocking down bowling pins, making good S1 judgments, our rational analysis might best be stashed in the trash less it interfere with feelings.[232] This kind of haste may not always make waste. Uncluttered feelings and emotions sometimes simplify the decision to stop or to go without a loss of accuracy. Nevertheless, we need to be sure we are not throwing out the baby with the bath water when we simplify the relevant information. What data we include or leave out depends on the questions we are trying to answer. Remembering the O-ring issues of the Challenger,

---

[230] K2011 pg 87 "It is the consistency of the information that matters for a good story, not its completeness."

[231] We make stories based on first impressions. Though we know this first meeting is a small sample of who the person is, we try to create a story based on that sample. The expressions 'you never get a second chance to make a first impression' and 'first impressions are the most lasting' speak to the weight as an anchor we value these impressions. With little information, we have a lot of liberty in creating the story, there are few bounds to our imagination. Often if someone is trying to make an impression, we need to keep in mind Chris Rock's comment that when you are meeting him for the first time, you are not meeting him, you are meeting his representative.

[232] I always saw better when my eyes were closed. Tom Waits

do we leave out the silent evidence of low O-ring defects at high temperature in order to analyze low temperature defects? Someone thought these high temperature/low damage results were peripheral to understanding O-ring low temperature/high damage results. They were wrong, these results were essential.

If we deliberately leave out information in the re-construction of the story, we must be careful not to eliminate data that provides important context, the baby with the bath water. We would also do well to remember that stories have lives of their own in that, like memories, they can be very flexible (open to reconstruction) while at the same time remaining internally consistent. Each time we call on our memory of a story, updates to the reconstruction of them can cause alterations to occur, usually to the benefit of story cohesiveness and/ or to enhance our own part in the story. Alterations can also reflect the inclusion of newly available information as if it had always been there as part of the original memory/ story. "Inconvenient details tend to be pruned from our memories, and facts that do not fit together in a coherent way tend to be forgotten, de-emphasized, or reinterpreted."[233]

The following experiment reported by Gigerenzer[234] shows how less information can lead to a better decision. This study was performed to improve (make a more true judgment) the decision making process of deciding where to send patients admitted to a hospital with chest pain. Historically 90% of such patients were admitted to the coronary care unit. These conservative, defensive decisions lead to overcrowding and poorer health care. Decision making improved when an expert system with 50 probabilities and logistic regression was adopted.

---

[233]   Hallinan pg 123

[234]   Gigerenzer Rationality pg 42/3

Nevertheless, doctors were wary of using a tool they didn't understand.

A simple decision tree was then tried with just a couple of questions. The first was, "Does the patient have an anomaly in his electrocardiogram". If yes, admit to the coronary care unit. If no, ask another specific question. A third and final question finished the process which turned out, despite a disregard of much patient information, to give better results than the physicians working either with or without the logistic regression instrument. Less information can be more accurate[235]. The art, as Gerd noted, is to ignore the right kind of information[236].

The fitness that our brains were built for has strongly valued adaptability and the ability to make speedy, robust decisions. Acquiring all the detailed truth can cost more time and effort than we can afford. It seems that we can't handle the truth. In a case of the best being the enemy of the good, if we can't close the deal with the information readily available, we may risk missing the opportunity to act, and so we get left behind, still searching for the best decision.

As simple as possible . . . but not any more so. Einstein

Data demise in story telling has several enablers including stereotyping, base rate neglect, and categorization.[237] These information simplifications sit well with CE. Since "our brains are made for fitness, not for truth"[238], we value getting assignments off our plates; we'll take speed at the expense of the facts. Decisions need to be made, and the degree of belief, the degree of truth

---

[235] Kate McGarry's album "If Less is More . . . Nothing is Everything"
[236] Gigerenzer Rationality pg 42
[237] Taleb Black prologue xxx
[238] Taleb random pg 197, and see also Schulz pg 337, ". . . . the goal of therapy isn't necessarily to make our beliefs more accurate, it's to make them more functional."

required, depends on the severity of problem at hand and our window of opportunity to act. For the inconsequential, little is needed. For a life or death decision, say, in a courtroom murder trial, the required degree of truth expected increases to beyond that of reasonable doubt. How much confidence we need depends on the urgency and consideration of the consequences. The stories we tell adjust to take into account the needs of the decision maker. We may just need to know who won. If we're betting with a spread, we also want to know by how much.

To reduce complexity and to add to our false sense of security, we create models that overly simplify. Part of these simplified models may include 'Platonification', the simplifying classification of information.

Taleb describes Platonicity[239] as" . . . our tendency to mistake the map for the territory, to focus on pure and well-defined forms . . . [240]" and [241] ". . . what makes us think that we understand more than we actually do." Platonicity is the practice of pigeonholing, putting information into overly accommodating, neat little boxes. This practice simplifies and tends to make a story more convincing than it really is. It supports model making by making little of the role of randomness. Since we do not play well with

---

[239] TalBlack pg 303 "Platonicity: the focus on those pure, well-defined, and easily discernible object like triangles, or more social notions like friendship or love, at the cost of ignoring those objects of seemingly messier and less tractable structures." We build or acquire models and patterns into which we expect reality to fit. As George Box wrote, "All models are wrong, some are more useful than others."

[240] Taleb Black pg xxix

[241] Taleb Black pg 15 "Categorizing is necessary for humans, but it becomes pathological when the category is seen as definitive, preventing people from considering the fuzziness of boundaries."

randomness, we make it virtually disappear into a Platonic[242] silo. Randomness is just another abstract statistical concept like the average. We do well inferring the general from the individual, but not vice versa. This leads into our overuse of the individual story to the exclusion of concepts of the general, such as statistics.

The quality of our decisions is affected by the quality of our available information, and quality of judgment is affected by sample size among other considerations. We are obliged to either disregard what a small sample tells us, or use it as a model for some future prediction. It's hard to disregard information even when it is neutral or known to be unreliable.

Actual content is something we tend to pay more importance to than quality of content.[243] This emphasis on content means we seldom make decisions that include critical but unknown (such as a base rate) information, and that comes from not knowing what we do not know, that, for example, the base rate and/or other information is needed.

For example, if we have a diagnostic test that is about 90% accurate, that is, the test correctly detects 90% of the patients who have the condition; we probably guess that if the test is positive, then there is about a 90% chance that the patient has the condition. Sounds reasonable, but the

---

[242] Plato believed in perfect never changing Forms, none of which could exist on this imperfect world. For example, tableness is the perfect form of any real table. For our purposes here, the Platonic silo is a mental compartment used to strip the item of its imperfections. We put the real world 'tables' which vary in and among themselves into these perfect characterizations. Rather than include the imperfect table in the story, it's imperfect, variable nature is removed by negating its variability. This often works well enough, but we must not forget its variability is real.

[243] K2011 pg 118 ". . . we pay more attention to the content of messages than to information about their reliability . . ."

answer to the problem requires knowing the rate of false positives and the base rate of the frequency of the condition in the population. We see a scenario of this problem worked out in Appendix 6, where the probability of a patient with the condition given that they had a positive test was not about 90%, but close to 20%. This was calculated based on the base rate of 1/1000 having the condition and the 5% chance that a patient not having the condition tests positive. This kind of 'silent' information that is often critical but unsought for, is necessary to correctly answer the original question of the how well this patient is, given a positive diagnostic test. See the Appendix 1 for the taxi cab and Appendix 2 for the birthday problem that serve as examples of how poor our intuition is in solving probability problems.

We rely on patterns or stories, to simplify information and to make it more memorable. Things that were not (perhaps incorrectly) identified as causal will be less likely to be incorporated in a model or explanation. Silent evidence (where nothing is happening), is silent for this very reason of its not being causal because nothing is happening and so nothing is being caused. Still, silent evidence is evidence and should be included in analyses using base rates, such as the non-eventful Challenger O-ring performance at high temperatures. As Bacon said, "The root of all superstition is that men observe when a thing hits, but not when it misses." The misses are the silent evidence[244]. This cherry picking, confirmatory approach has limited applicability in scientific methodology. Oversight rather than overlooking is the approach that gains the hypothesis credibility. If the pattern survives the search for disconfirming evidence, the story will be that much more convincing.

---

[244]   Taleb Black pg 121 "Out of sight, out of mind: we harbor a natural, even physical, scorn of the abstract." WYSIATI

Opposite to the problem of extremely small sample size, we are numbed by large numbers and their averages, probabilities, or distributions. As a consequence, unfortunately, we find it more difficult to deduce the individual from the general, as this was apparently not an evolutionary requirement.[245] The bias to greater familiarity with the use of small numbers leads to greater reliance on them and to more undue confidence, and so greater CE, our goal.

Believing is seeing

We are wired to perceive and believe, not to doubt.

We do not see things as they are; we see things as we are. Even the process of vision includes a subjective part where we 'interpret' visual signals. Babies see the world upside down until the brain adjusts. If you wear glasses that invert the image for a sufficient period of time for your brain to adjust, you too will see the world upside down when you remove them. Magicians or 'illusionists' take advantage of the structure and limitations of our visual processing to trick our minds. Visual Illusions are proof that our minds can change what is perceived, even while the object being seen is not changing.

Another example of this is found in the Kuleshov effect where the sight of an unchanging expressionless person is paired with different pictures that influence our interpretations of who this person is or what they are thinking. After being shown with a bowl of soup, he was

---

[245] Gigerenzer Risks pg 37 "Why is it so difficult for even highly educated people to make inferences on the basis of probabilities? The fact that the notion of mathematical probability developed so late- later than most key philosophical concepts has been called the "*scandal of philosophy*"

judged to be pensive; after being shown with a dead woman, he was judged to be sorrowful. Our beliefs change when context changes. Rorschach ink blot tests are designed to take advantage of this heuristic need for consistency and coherence in order to interpret our personality.

The default bias of believing that something is true, takes less work than skeptically doubting. An experiment[246] was conducted where subjects were shown a number of nonsensical assertions each of which were followed by one of the words "True" or "False". They were tested later to determine how well they remembered these associations. When their S2 was manipulated to be busy in this test by having the subjects retain a number in their memory, the subjects optimistically reported more of the "False" associations to be "True". This may be explained by the theory (Spinoza's conjecture) that first you must understand what the consequences are of believing a statement to be true before it can be judged by S2 to be not true. If the S2 is busy, the default of belief does not get sufficiently evaluated to be changed to disbelief where appropriate. From an evolutionary perspective, this bias makes sense in that your experiences are by nature true, though nature can be deceitful. You believe what you feel, good or bad. Type 2 errors that determined patterns to be false when in fact they are true are not survivor friendly (see the bear in a bush discussion). As a result, we tend to believe what is more easily imagined (a red block) than the more difficult imagining of a non-event (a not red block). If we tend to be gullible, it's because it takes less work to believe than to be skeptical.

"You can see why assuming causality could have had evolutionary advantages. It is part of the general vigilance that we have inherited from ancestors."[247]

---

[246]   K2011, pg 81
[247]   K2011 pg 115

The stories (cause and effect) we make up can be coherent but need not necessarily be true. For example[248] "All roses are flowers, some flowers fade quickly, therefore some roses fade quickly." At first this conclusion seems reasonable, and was deemed valid by a large majority of the college students to whom it was presented. Just because "all roses are flowers, some flowers fade quickly", it does not necessarily (*therefore*) follow that some roses fade quickly. That this conclusion was jumped at seems to indicate that we are a little lazy and we don't check our answers.

What you don't know . . .

How would you feel about allowing your teen-age daughter to go to a rock/rap concert for the first time?[249] "You may know that there is really (almost) nothing to worry about, but you cannot help images and anecdotes of bad things from coming to mind. As Slovic has argued, the amount of concern is not adequately sensitive to the probability of harm; you are imagining the numerator—the tragic story you saw on the news-and not thinking about the denominator [the non-events]." "Denominator neglect" [Slovic] is a label used for this kind of thinking for which Sunstein has coined the phrase "probability neglect". What you don't know can hurt you.

Again, we prioritize content of information over its quality and at times this prioritization is done to the exclusion of the consideration of the quality of the information. This can result in insensitivity to sample size (an element of information quality) which we can default define as 1 (one[250]) for an individual story or anecdote.

---

[248]   K2011 pg 45

[249]   K2011pg144

[250]   Data is not the plural of anecdote

Confidence in a small sample size as representative of a larger distribution of values is addressed more generally by Kahneman who claims: "The exaggerated faith in small samples is only one example of a more general illusion—we pay more attention to the content of messages than to information about their reliability, and as a result wind up with a view of the world around us that is simpler and more coherent than the data justify."[251] "System 1 is radically insensitive to both the quality and quantity of the information that gives rise to impressions and intuitions."[252]

"System 1 excels at constructing the best possible story that incorporates ideas currently activated, but it does not (cannot) allow for information it does not have." "The amount and quality of the data on which the story is based are largely irrelevant"[253] ". . . participants who saw one-sided evidence were more confident of their judgments than those who saw both sides. This is just what you would expect if the confidence that people experience is determined by the coherence of the story they manage to construct from available information. It is the consistency of the information that matters for a good story, not its completeness. Indeed, you will often find that knowing little makes it easier to fit everything you know into a coherent pattern."[254]

A continuing theme throughout this book is that most of the decisions we make come from our unconscious S1 system. S1 encompasses our feelings, our intuition, our emotions. It gives us a sense of what to do, without taking time to rationalize. It is quick to fulfill its purpose of monitoring the environment for danger, resources, and reproductive opportunities. S1 presents the results of

---

[251] Kahneman 2011 pg 118
[252] K2011 pg 86
[253] K2011 pg 85
[254] K2011 pg 87

its sensing activity to S2. When time is available and your rational mind is in a comfortable place, we (S2) can build on the rough drafts that S1 has provided by engineering a story to support or negate our gut feelings. Otherwise, without S2 we have to let S1 go it alone and trust its intuitive auto pilot.

Why do we need stories?

A story, for our purposes, is any convenient device that explains and integrates those collections of components that are our senses, feelings, and memories into a whole that helps achieve purposes such as providing a way to understand our feelings, resolve dissonances, or facilitate memory.[255] Sometimes when struggling to recall an actor's name, we search for things that may be related, hoping we will stumble upon it. Until we get closure, we say it's on the tip of the tongue, and it's driving us crazy. Our minds play an internal game of charades where we try verbal and non-verbal hints to elicit a word or phrase. When the sought after word or phrase is found, it will tie together all of the associated hints. Consider the following.

---

[255] Taleb Black pg 70 "But memory and the arrow of time can get mixed up. Narrativity can viciously affect the remembrance of past events as follows: we will tend to more easily remember those facts from our past that fit a narrative, while we tend to neglect others that do not appear to play a causal role in the narrative. Consider that we recall events in our memory all the while knowing the answer of what happened subsequently. It is literally impossible to ignore posterior information when solving a problem. This simple inability to remember not the true sequence of events but a reconstructed one will make history appear in hindsight to be far more explainable than it actually was—or is."

"A newspaper is better than a magazine. A sea shore is a better place than the street. At first it is better to run than to walk. You may have to try several times. It takes some skill, but is easy to learn. Even your children can enjoy it. Once successful, complications are minimal. Birds seldom get too close. Rain, however, soaks in very fast. Too many people doing the same thing can also cause problems. One needs lots of room. If there are no complications, it can be very peaceful. A rock will serve as an anchor. If things break loose from it, however, you will not get a second chance."[256]

Something is missing, there doesn't seem to be a unifying thread. What do these ideas have in common? I'm thinking you're thinking, 'not much'. Did the word 'kite' come to mind? If not, read it again. Note that by adding the missing piece of the puzzle, we have united the details of the paragraph into a story more easily remembered. Paradoxically, the addition of information, since it served to tie loose ends together, resulted in less work to remember. This collection of sentences became a story when 'kite' was added.

The tension of not knowing pushes us to find, if not the answer, at least an answer. By uniting the components within a story, we achieve a higher level of cognitive ease. Uncomfortable doubt is resolved.

We want to believe, and sometimes even a hint of an explanatory connection gives us some comfort. Palm readers take advantage of this need for creating stories. The discomfort of not knowing why, drives us to find structure in a world of noise. We find patterns where there are none,[257]

---

[256] Burton pg 5

[257] Paulos pg 29 As an example of how much we need to assign causes: "A simple experiment . . . illustrates how the difference between the objects in two sets—presumably people in two groups-can be exaggerated simply by labeling them: Four lines are labeled A, while four slightly longer lines are labeled B. People think the differences in length between the lines in the

even when applying risk analysis graphical tools such as control charts and histograms to find patterns in a sea of noise. We have trouble recognizing noise as being just data caused by random independent factors. Our intuitions rely heavily on the sense of pattern recognition. Even when randomness is the true explanation for a sequence of events, we often capture it in illusory patterns that in turn affect our behavior. See Chapter 3 where coin flips appeared more random if some of the randomness was removed. The effect was also found by the Apple Company on a shuffle feature that was applied to their i-pods. Enough complaints were made about the lack of randomness that the Apple CEO, Steve Jobs, was convinced that since the customer was always right and so, "We made it less random to make it feel more random." [258] As easily as we see faces and animals in the clouds, we see patterns in random data. There's a name for this: Pareidolia[259]

Cognitive Ease

When the limited resources of System 2 don't allow for a checkpoint filtration of the System 1 stories,[260] those same stories gain more power to convince on a gut level. When this happens, the rules of logic and rationality fade off the radar. Without this control, System 1 and its heuristics can

---

two sets are bigger than do people presented with the same lines unlabeled. Similar judgments of difference persist when the average length of the lines in the two groups is adjusted to be the same." A neutral label should not affect our decision.

[258] Lehrer pg 66

[259] Pareidolia is a psychological phenomenon involving a vague and random stimulus (often an image or sound) being perceived as significant.

[260] K2011 pg 41 "System 1 has more influence on behavior when System 2 is busy."

lead to the biases we have already discussed, and more. For example, in an experiment where words associated with pictures were shown for a period of time that was too short for System 2 to acknowledge seeing anything, it was later shown that those elements that were shown more frequently were later described more favorably than the rest. Though we are not conscious of the pictures, we react according to the heuristic that biases us to be more comfortable with things we familiar with. This story of familiarity leading to favorableness translates into CE. It also serves as a hook in many songs. How much you like the song probably is influenced in part by how often you listen to it or the frequency of repetitions of a phrase/chorus in the song.

"The mere exposure effect does not depend on the conscious experience of familiarity. In fact, the effect does not depend on consciousness at all: it occurs even when the repeated words or pictures are shown so quickly that the observers never become aware of having seen them. They still end up liking the words of pictures that were presented more frequently. As should be clear by now, System 1 can respond to impressions of events of which System 2 is unaware. Indeed, the mere exposure effect is actually stronger for stimuli that the individual never consciously sees."[261] "The link between positive emotion and cognitive ease in System 1 has a long evolutionary history."[262]

"Cognitive fluency [ease] refers to our brains' tendency to accept messages that are easy to understand and effortlessly fit into existing schemata—and, when positively employed, it is a skill crucial to learning. The reason that persuasive messages are short, pithy, and digestible in seconds is that we process them so quickly that they become familiar without us even noticing."[263]

---

[261]   K2011 pg 67
[262]   K2011 pg 67
[263]   Disalvo pg 155

Our Creative Minds[264]

Our narratives sometimes depend on getting creative with what we think we heard. If you didn't hear the words well, make up something to fill the gap. The sense of hearing is not exempt from using its creativity to re-work words that weren't heard well. Because we need to feel that we understand, we prefer to unconsciously make up replacement words rather than leave a blank. Yesterday a co-worker thanked me for some checklists. I thought she was thanking me for Chiclets. Consider the example from the book The World According to Garp where the son understood that the father had warned him about the Under Toad, when the father was actually warning him about the under tow. Musical lyrics also have a history of being misunderstood. Take the song Purple Haze by Jimi Hendrix. There is a Kissthisguy website of misheard lyrics, stating that the correct lyrics are 'scuse me while I kiss the sky'. I had always thought it was kiss the sky until I saw him in concert. Something about his gestures that made me think that line was referring to the bass player. Or take Black Sabbath, where I heard ". . . they will fill your head with lice . . ." though it was they will fill your head with lies.

We work with our speedy S1 to push whatever pops into our S2 head. Getting it wrong could be funny, or it could be dangerous.

Think of how more than one interpretation can be made for each of the following.

I saw the man with the binoculars
Police help dog bite victim.
They are hunting dogs.
Put the box on the table in the kitchen

---

[264] Teacher to parent: "The good news is your child has a lot of creative ideas. The bad news is they are all in spelling." Or was it memory . . . ?

Our non-conscious system will send these statements to S2 without any interpretation, without any ambiguity. S2 will play with context to try to determine which meaning had the true intent. This need for determination assumes that we are aware that a syntactic ambiguity is present and needs to be resolved. No doubt some of these erroneous interpretations will make it into our stories, so beware. "System 1 is not prone to doubt. It suppresses ambiguity and spontaneously constructs stories that are as coherent as possible."[265]

Another example of our creative minds,

"After spending a day exploring the beautiful sights in the crowded streets of New York, Jane discovered that her wallet was missing."[266]

When subjects were given a recall test after reading this story, they associated the word "pickpocket" with it more often than "sights", even though "sights" was included in the story and "pickpocket" was not. This is illustrative of how we interact with stories. We search for closure, the warm 'why' and fuzzy 'because'. We look for associative coherence as one rule in the making of the story. Other explanations for the missing wallet may have been just as valid, but System 1 is not looking for the best story, just one that can be pieced together quickly. If that can't be done, System 2 kicks in and a slower, more analytical approach takes over the role of story making.

Just like the Dude's rug that tied his room together,[267] a word that associates New York's crowded streets with the loss of a wallet is "pickpocket", and that word ties the story together. We're satisfied, we don't look any further.

For the purpose of understanding how we make decisions, stories can be very influential, especially if they

---

[265]   K2011 pg 114
[266]   K2011 pg 75
[267]   The Big Lebowski movie, 1998

make sense and are consistent. System 1 makes stories that flow from one moment to another, and so by nature are generally cohesive. Interruptions in that cohesiveness should set off an internal alarm. Like fire alarms, the alarm level varies with the resources that might be needed. System 1 receives sensory input and quickly converts it into usable information in the form of feelings and intuition. It is not prone to doubt, so its stories are biased to favor certainty.

The need for certainty ties in with the well worn humor in response to a complicated explanation that you really didn't understand is "I knew that." We do want to feel that we know so much it's laughable. That poor excuse for an explanation, randomness, is low on the list of possible causes. Using randomness as an explanation can feel like no explanation at all and so our reluctance to invoke it. Randomness kills certainty.

System 2 gets involved in deciding if there is a logical association of ideas which would indicate coherence. If the story is lacking, S2 may fill in the missing elements, crystallizing around a concept such as the kite, rug, or pickpocket. Once we have a story that convinces us of a certain viewpoint, we are unlikely to be swayed by new and contradictory information. This is even more unlikely if the new stuff is presented in a different (statistical vs. story format[268]) from that which you were originally convinced. If you are satisfied with 'kite', you are unlikely to continue to look for a better explanation. It takes another story to supersede a story you've already been convinced of. If your belief is based in science, an anecdote will probably not change your position. It will probably take another scientific argument to do that.

We make stories based on first impressions. Though we know this first meeting is a small sample of who the person is, we try to create a story based on that sample.

---

[268] Taleb, it takes a story to replace a story.

The expressions 'you never get a second chance to make a first impression' and 'first impressions are the most lasting' speak to the weight as an anchor that we value these impressions.

Good news, bad news and our body of knowledge

The continual vigilance of System 1, where there is a constant awareness and reporting of the immediate surroundings, resonates with its evolutionary past where, as they say with good reason, 'bad news travels quickly.' So quickly in fact, that if a source of danger is presented to you that is sufficiently brief, you can physically react to it even though you aren't conscious that it was presented to you. You know more than you know you know. In experiments where a threatening picture was presented to a subject for less than 2/100 of a second, the subjects reported that they were unaware of it, yet their amygdalas, considered the brain's "threat center", lit up under the scanner. The same experiment with non threatening observations had no effect on the amygdala.[269] Good news doesn't sell as well. Good news is a nice to have, but is usually not as urgent as the news that you have suddenly become some predator's prey. Evolutionary Rule #1, stay alive, tune in to the threatening stories, put the rest on the backburner.

This unconscious perception of the world colors our narratives. In particular, our mental associations can affect our feelings in a way that influences the acceptability of a

---

[269] K2011 pg 301, "The brain responds quickly even to purely symbolic threats. Emotionally loaded words quickly attract attention, and bad words (war, crime) attract attention faster than do happy words (peace, love). There is no real threat, but the mere reminder of a bad event is treated in System 1 as threatening."

story.[270] Reading the kite story was an uncomfortable activity since it was incomplete, not cohesive. You felt there had to be more, and this feeling originates in the unconscious.

Miracles and superstition—stories we use for the inexplicable.

In an unpredictable environment, we are more likely to accept casual relations when we need causal ones. "It is interesting to note that lacking control increases what is called illusory pattern recognition. When individuals are induced to feel a lack of control, they are more likely to see meaningful patterns in random data. They are responding to their unfortunate lack of control by generating (false) coherence in data that would then help them feel they have greater control."[271] This kind of superstitious thinking can exert an insidious effect in shaping a story.

"Miracles do not happen in contradiction to nature, but only in contradiction to that which is known to us of nature."[272] Saint Augustine (354-430)

We sports fans are not exempted from inventing stories to explain the unknown. In uncertain times, like in close games, we reach for explanations (how could we have lost?) and by the nature of uncertainty (it's usually not well

---

[270] Herbert pg 29, "We 'see' the world through the lens of our emotions". While we tend to overestimate cliff heights (when looking from above the cliff), those with a fear of heights judge the height of a cliff as being higher than those without that fear. This is another example of heuristic induced bias. Feelings come first, explanations follow.

[271] Trivers pg 23

[272] Paulos pg 62 "Hume observed that every piece of evidence for a miraculous coincidence—that is, for a violation of natural law—is also evidence of the proposition that the regularities the alleged miracle violated are not laws of nature after all."

understood nor evaluated), our stories concerning it tend to underestimate how poor our explanations are. Sports and gambling have a rich history of players continuing to do what was done when a win happened. To win again we feel obliged to wear the same socks we wore when we won the big game. The superstitious mind easily converts a spurious association into a causal relationship. We like to think we have control, and so too easily we determine correlations to be causations. Our use of the term 'story' to include explanations and predictions also includes superstition as a tool to get to cognitive ease.

No doubt the 1972 championship game between the Oakland Raiders and the Pittsburgh Steelers spurred a number of superstitious behaviors. The game had been a hard fought defensive battle. The score was 7 to 6 with Oakland in the lead. With 22 seconds left to play, fourth down and ten yards from a first down and 60 yards from a touchdown, Steeler quarterback Terry Bradshaw evaded a tackle then launched a pass down field. The ball somehow bounced backwards from the intended receiver or the defensive player back to rookie Franco Harris who took it in for a score and the championship. In a profession given to exaggeration, calling this play "The greatest miracle in sports history", the "Miraculous Reception" is worth a look on You Tube to see why many believe it deserves its title. This play marked a turnaround in Steeler fortunes, some would claim, because the superstitions that were born that day influenced fan behavior (and supposedly team success) for years to come. As a current TV commercial states about superstitious behavior, "It's only weird if it doesn't work."

Superstitions arise out of our need for control. Subjects were presented with either a horizontal or vertical row of lights. Before each trial, they were asked to predict which would be the result. When the sequence was random, their responses were about 50/50, but a repeat of the prediction for either was more probable if their previous answer was correct. If correctly predicted twice in a row, they repeated the prediction 72% of the time, though the probability remained 50% of getting that third in a row. They thought they saw a pattern where there was none, and acted like this information could help them predict better.[273]

Superstitions are stories that are usually meant as a precautionary tales, while miracles are those (good) events or coincidences that seem highly unlike what would be expected from nature taking her usual course. In the Steelers story, for the Oakland fans, this play might better be remembered as the Debaculous (if I may coin a word that captures some of the controversy of that play, which I will not go into) Reception. Both superstitions and miracles may rely on our poor sense of randomness. We want to impose patterns on everything, including randomness, which, by definition, is devoid of patterns.

Superstitions can arise from our lack of understanding of how an effect was caused. Wade Boggs, one of major league's best hitters, was said to always eat chicken the day of a game. That practice was considered to be superstitious, but it might just as well have been his way of staying away from less healthy food that might cause some discomfort during the ensuing game. Since his hitting was so consistently good, there were many opportunities for a good game to follow a meal of chicken. Wade had a superstitious personality, especially about the number 17. From the time he woke to the number of practice ground balls he fielded, the number 17 could be found. Whatever the actual story, the relation was eventually fixed as a habit. One less thing to think about, one more simplification to remove the chore of choice.

If our model is poor at predicting, we might simplify with a miracle as Sydney Harris did in one of his cartoons, where, in the midst of a complicated equation on the black

---

[273] Plouse pg 157

board appear the words, "Then a miracle happens". His cartoon colleague comments "I think you should be more explicit here in step two." A similar thinking occurs in a Gary Larsen cartoon where two cavemen remark on a huge mastodon lain slain by a tiny arrow. One comments, "Maybe we should write that spot down" (where the arrow hit). The arrow probably had little to do the creature's demise, but it would be nice to take credit for this once in a lifetime coincidence, and so the humor. The probability of future failure to down a similarly sized animal in spite of the hit being 'on spot' are probably pretty good. However, those that believe hitting the target works miracles (it apparently did for one of them) will re-interpret failure of future results as being due to not being sufficiently accurate. This conjecture works in the same path as some self-help books that promise great things if you believe enough. If the great things don't come, it's because you did not believe enough. Your arrow was not accurate enough; you didn't hit the 'true' spot. This is an example of why it is said that businesses may come and go, but religion and the market for self-help books will last forever, for in no other endeavor does the consumer blame himself for product failure.

From Shermer's book, "The evolutionary rationale for superstition is clear: natural selection will favor strategies that make many incorrect causal associations in order to establish those that are essential for survival and reproduction."[274]

Evolution has supported these 'just so' stories as part of the fallout of its bias towards generally accepting stories. Some of these stories establish associations despite the dearth of true supporting elements. In response we fill in any holes of our story with more ad hoc excuses. We use superstition, deceit, and a touch of the miraculous to fill in the missing pieces. To our creative satisfaction,

---

[274] Shermer pg 62

we have succeeded in Rube Goldberging our way to a convincing, if not self-deceiving, story. We struggle with the delicate balance between being skeptical enough to critically challenge new hypotheses, and letting down that guard to be open to new, perhaps previous not well thought out alternative models. "With this evolutionary perspective we can now understand that people believe weird things because of our evolved need to believe nonweird things."[275]These 'weird' things we believe come in handy for the stories we tell. Superstitions, broadly defined as irrational couplings of cause and effect, are useful in presenting a convincing story especially when the superstition is a shared belief.

Continuing with Shermer, ". . . we tend to find meaningful patterns whether they are there or not, and there are a perfectly good reason to do so. In this sense, patternicities (the tendency for finding patterns) derived from thinking as superstition and magical thinking are not so much errors in cognition as they are natural processes of a learning brain. We can no more eliminate superstitious learning that we can eliminate all learning. Although true pattern recognition helps us survive, false pattern recognition does not necessarily get us killed, and so the patternicity phenomenon endured the winnowing process of natural selection. Because we must make associations in order to survive and reproduce, natural selection favored all association-making strategies, even those that resulted in false positives."

Check out the following URL: http://www.onemorelevel. com/game/amazing_mind_reader. The magic in the mind reader can be explained with a little effort, or we can be lazy and believe the result is due to magic.

How do superstitions get started? Superstition seems to come to us very naturally. Once my boss told me it was

---

[275] Shermer pg 62

bad luck to change the month of the calendar before the month changes. I suspect that he was just passing along someone else's comments or just made it up on the spot. We had been talking about spooky coincidences a short time before this. It brought to mind a superstition I came up with several years ago that apparently never caught on. An avocado had rolled off the counter and fell on the floor in abuela's home. Avocados bruise easily and I thought if it fell again it might ruin the avocado, so I said, tongue in cheek, "They say it's bad luck if you drop an avocado twice." The reaction was along the lines of 'I've never heard that, where did you learn it?' I had expected a little more skepticism like 'You're making that up, right?' I guess my straight face and lack of history for practical jokes made this one a little less unbelievable. We want to believe. Also, like the stories you hear on April Fool's day, "falsehoods live in the neighborhood of truth and so more easily delude us." My contrived superstition was harmless since it was in the 'neighborhood of truth', and I tried to send the superstitious yet didactic message to be careful when handling avocados. I suspect many superstitions originated as good advice. We are biased to believe, and that is consistent with our evolutionary need to find patterns which, when successful, give us a little more predictive power.

Let's go back to the Larson cartoon where two cavemen are discussing the killing of a mighty mammoth, where a tiny arrow had dropped the beast. There is humor in the absurdity of the presumed effect a small arrow had, felling the mammoth. Had this scene not been cartoon in nature, but actually true, we would all want to know the cause of the little arrow's potency. What story could we make to explain what happened, especially with a look to predicting the future. This cartoon quote ("Maybe we should write this spot down.") assumes the power of the arrow to fell this huge animal lies in its location where the arrow lodged. We may conclude that the event is so wonderful and so rare, that all we can do is take the easy way out and say is that it must have been a miracle. The individual who made the shot is probably thinking that the key ingredient was the individual who made the shot. We take advantage of the lack of understanding to take credit for the success.

One of my favorite superstitions comes from the book The Rainbow by Carl Boyer. In it he recounts a myth from the Kaitish tribe of Central Australia, who ". . . believe that the rainbow is the son of the rain, and that with filial regard he is anxious to prevent his father from falling to the earth. Hence if the rainbow appears in the sky at a time when rain is wanted, they try to enchant the bow away." My take on this is that if you see a rainbow, there is likely to be associated moisture, likely rain, that is yet to come or already has come to pass.

No matter what you do, the rainbow will go eventually away and you will likely experience the much needed rain. This superstition "works", and its origin may either have been a single event or several experienced over time. The origin of this path from the casual to the causal is often lost to history.

Making a story believable brings us a step closer to the goal of CE. Where there is ambiguity there is discomfort. The dissonant nature of ambiguity needs to be resolved to make our stories effective. By accentuating the positive, and rejecting the negative, we feel good and are more likely to accept the story as true. "So powerful is our tendency to rationalize that contrary evidence is often immediately greeted with criticism, distortion, and dismissal so that not much dissonance needs to be suffered, nor change of opinion required."[276] Neutral information can become more familiar, more positive, with time and repetition.

---

[276] Trivers pg 153

Rhyme or songs also make the story more memorable. Advertisements use these tools to get into your head. You're not buying a car; you're buying a dream machine that will take you to the ends of the earth with your fine companion. Zoom Zoom

Depending on how a problem is presented (framed), our choice between equivalent scenarios may change. For example[277] whether the story is framed positively or negatively will affect your decision on how to act. In the following scenario, you are informed that a new form of a disease is about to reach the U.S. Six hundred are expected to die if no action is taken. Do you take action 'A' that will save 200 of these lives, or do you take the risk of action 'B' where there is a 1/3 possibility that all 600 will be saved. The affect heuristic kicks in and you consider the regret you will feel if the 2/3 possibility that all 600 will be lost, comes to fruition. Despite the essential equivalence of 'A' and 'B', 72% choose 'A'. In a second framing of the situation, plan C results in 400 deaths. This is functionally equivalent to plan 'A', but in A we speak of lives saved, in C, deaths. For Plan D there is a 1/3 probability that all will survive (a 2/3 probability that all will die). We choose D over C even though they are equivalent. Actually all four plans are equivalent, but we are biased to avoid risks unless we take them to avoid losses.

Our decision to take a risk or not depends our choice of frame. For A and B the frame is lives saved. We take chances to avoid losses, but these two choices are not framed as losses, but as lives saved. For C and D the frame is lives lost and we will take chances to avoid losses. This seems like a flimsy justification[278], but is consistent with the Framing heuristic. "The operations of associative memory

---

277   Shermer pg 269 (see also Baron pg269)
278   The heart has arguments [*heuristics*] with which the logic of the mind is not acquainted. Blaise Pascal.

contribute to a general confirmation bias. When asked, 'Is Sam friendly?' different instances of Sam's behavior will come to mind than would if you had been asked 'Is Sam unfriendly?'[279] Would you be more likely to buy from Store A, which advertised "Discount for cash" or Store B, which advertised "Charge for credit?" We are less likely to choose hamburger labeled "15% fat" than one that reads "85% lean". A poll reported on NPR Sep 27, 2013 reads 48% against Obama Care and 37% against the Affordable Health Care Act. The 'popular' name is the same act as the official name. This is the anti-Obama bias at work. In the 2013 Nov/Dec Scientific American, pg16, "When physicians rephrased 'do not resuscitate' as 'allow natural death,' family members opted for the latter 27.5% more often. It was found that choice of metaphor changed subject's behavior. In one study it was found that if a participant read "Crime is a virus", the reaction was to apply a systematic approach to reducing crime. If the participant read "Crime is a beast", the reaction was towards a more direct approach emphasizing enforcement.

The deliberate search for confirming evidence, know as positive test strategy, is also how System 2 often supports a hypothesis. Contrary to the practice of philosophers of science, who advise testing hypotheses by trying to refute them, people seek data that are likely to be compatible with the beliefs they currently hold.

In a another experiment[280], subjects chose between (A) a sure gain of $240, and (B) a 25% chance to gain $1000. Eighty-four percent chose A. Being risk averse is like preferring "a bird in the hand" to two in the bush. We are more likely to take risks to avoid losses, than take risks to achieve gains.

---

[279] K2011 pg 81
[280] Plous pg 70

Subjects were then asked to chose between (C) a sure loss of $750, and (D) a 75% chance to lose $1000. Where losses could be reduced, we gamble. Seventy-three percent chose D.

In a life and death example, physicians had to choose between surgery and radiation to treat a condition. For the option of surgery, they were shown either (A) The one month survival rate is 90% or (B) There is a 10% mortality in the first month. 84% of physicians shown (A) chose surgery, 50% those shown (B) opted for surgery. Identical information leading to different decisions based on framing.[281]

One group of subjects is told that a parked car has rolled into and damaged a traffic sign. Another group is told that a parked car has rolled into and injured a pedestrian. The members of the first group generally view that event as an accident; the second group is more likely to hold the driver responsible. Other studies confirm that the more emotionally fraught an event or phenomenon is, the more eagerly people search for a story to make sense of it.

In a related article "The Act Defines the Victim" in the same aforementioned SciAm magazine (SAMind 24, 12 (2013), evaluations of the victim depended on the intention of the perpetrator. For example the group that heard an event where an unintentional act occurred, estimates of damage were about $2,700 vs. the true cost of 2,800. The estimated cost of the damage from the group that understood the diversion was intentional gave an estimate of just over $5,000.[282]

---

[281] K2011 pg 367

[282] "The findings have implications for our understanding of complex moral issues such as abortion. People may consider fetuses to be mentally aware because they think abortion is immoral—not the other way around. 'People often have knee-jerk moral intuitions and only come up with explanations of these intuitions after the fact," says co-author Adrian Ward,

Scientific American 11/12 2013, "Dirty Money Appeals More to the Righteous". Money could be earned from an ethically dubious source. Those who were asked to recall a past good deed were more likely to work harder for this tainted cash. ". . . individuals who had been asked to recall a virtuous act completed roughly 40 percent more tasks to earn the supposedly corrupt cash than their less morally reassured counterparts." It's as though we make moral deposits from time to time that we can draw on when faced with moral decisions.

These examples send the message that the stories we use to convince ourselves that we have made the right decision, are sometimes based more on feelings and emotions than on logical considerations.

Error in prediction

There are two basic kinds of error[283] we can make in testing our hypotheses / stories. There are two ways our model of the world could be wrong. If the world contains a certain element (say, a bear in a bush), and our model of the world doesn't, that's a Type 2 error. If the world does not contain a certain element and our model does, that's a type 1 error. Does your model of the rustling bush include the possibility that the rustling might be caused by a bear? If it does, it will be prone to type 1 error

In the courtroom, having committed a Type 2 error means that a guilty person goes free. Type 1 error occurs

---

a psychologist now at the University of Colorado at Boulder. "Many times apparent causal reasoning is simply post hoc justification.'"

[283] A third one is found in the use of heuristics where questions are sometimes substituted for the original, more of which was covered in the chapter on heuristics.

CHAPTER 5

when we make the incorrect judgment of guilty under the presumption (null hypothesis) of innocence. We are adverse to Type 1 errors in the court because besides wrongfully judging an innocent as guilty, the actual guilty party is still out there. Repeating the words of William Blackstone (1723:1780), "All presumptive evidence of felony should be admitted cautiously: for the law holds, that it is better that ten guilty people escape, that one innocent suffer."[284] Better to be gullible and assume the accused is innocent until there is evidence beyond reasonable doubt to the contrary. In the court, making a type 2 error is preferable to making a type 1 mistake.

Type 1 error in a medical diagnostic leads us to worry unnecessarily, while Type 2 occurs when we should have worried, but didn't. Type 1 error is a false alarm. Type 2 error is a false negative, which here means you were given a clean bill of health, but you were actually sick. Type 1 error indicates you are sick when you aren't. If this error leads to dangerous follow-up such as surgery, it could be more worrisome than Type 2 errors.

Since these kinds of errors cannot be eliminated, we work to weight (like a teeter toter) the risks in the Type 1 /2 arenas to make the favored kind of error more likely which as a consequence makes the less favored one less likely. The arguments of our legal system's story presume a null hypothesis of innocence. Assuming innocence, lawyers create their narratives to either draw the line or question where the line is, where a guilty verdict is beyond a reasonable doubt. This requires proving that a subject is guilty, not proof that he is innocent. Proof of innocence, proof that the null hypothesis is correct, requires interminable amounts of evidence. Proof of guilt, rejecting the null hypothesis, can be much easier to achieve. Easier, but it still must pass the beyond that criteria of reasonable

---

[284] Baron pg 233

doubt. "No amount of experimentation can ever prove me right; a single experiment can prove me wrong." Einstein

It takes effort to suspect, to disbelieve. Letting down your guard, your skepticism is easier than keeping it up. This may be true in part to Spinoza's conjecture[285] that prior to disbelief we need to first understand the belief in order to subsequently disbelieve it.

"A number of other critical aspects of the gap between statistics citing and storytelling derive from the fact that, as the proverbial writing teacher's maxim enjoins, a story shows, rather than tells. Stories may employ dialogue and other devices and do not limit themselves to declarative pronouncements; they develop the context and relevant relationships instead of merely positing raw data; they are open-ended and metaphorical, whereas statistics and mathematics generally are determinate and literal; and stories unfold in time instead of being presented as timeless."[286]

Depending upon our experience and levels of skepticism/gullibility, our perception of risk is acted on or ignored. We make a story either to go on alert or we just keep walking. If we experience the same dicey situation a few times without harm, our perception, our reality, our model of normality, our story adjusts (gets habituated) so as to not to become alarmed when it occurs again in the future. We learn a new normal. Here is one of those occasions that a certain amount of forgetfulness may be our ally in that it allows some flexibility in our actions by allowing us to learn with less unlearning, less competition from old, perhaps entrenched and worn out, ideas. See the April/May 2013 edition of Scientific American Mind for the study that seems to support the importance of being able

---

[285] How Mental Systems Believe, American Psychologist, Vol 46, No 2, February 1991 pgs 107 - 119

[286] Paulos pg 23

to forget in order to update with new memories. Adults have high levels of a protein (NR2A) that prevents such forgetting as shown in a study that mice were engineered to have more of this protein, seemed to have more trouble forming long-term memories.

As we've already discussed, besides the event we need to consider non-events. In the Larsen cartoon of the wonderment of two cavemen observing the downed giant with the little arrow, before we claim cause and effect, we should ask questions like 'How often has this story played out before, that is, how many times has that small arrow landed in that same spot and when that happens how often has it resulted in a kill?' What was the state of health of the animal? Was it already near death? Has one arrow in some other spot happened with the same happy result? Was the arrow doctored with a poison? To quote Bacon again, "The root of all superstition is that men observe when a thing hits, but not when it misses."

In **gambling**, we over celebrate our wins feeding the false impression that we can defeat the house, and so we under weight our losses as just bad luck. Making winners obvious with flashing lights and ringing bells deceives the innocent bystanders into thinking they can win as well. As Homer Simpson explained to his wife Marg why he was sure to win at gambling, he explained that he had something the other gamblers didn't, "a feeling". This kind of self deception to expose ourselves to risky behavior can certainly take us places we might not otherwise go and do what we otherwise might not. However, because we are prone to believing the positive, especially about ourselves We feel better, more confident, more at ease, even when the situation might not warrant it. Confidence in ourselves allows us to take more risks. We think we can beat the odds and sometimes we do. That 'sometimes' type of reinforcement is a strong behavior shaper.

Self Deception

> You've got to accentuate the positive
> Eliminate the negative
> And latch on to the affirmative
> Don't mess with Mister In-Between
>
> Johnny Mercer 1940's musical hit

Similar to the effects of superstitious thinking, deceit and self-deception have parts to play in our stories. On almost a daily basis celebrities are found cheating and athletes are found juicing. Cars are sold with hidden defects. Political promises are made knowing they cannot be fulfilled. In spite of the potential cost of deception being found out, it happens. Consequences of deceit are getting or giving something for less than the probable subsequent costs. You may mislead to get something tangible such as votes or home runs at the cost of your future or you may tell a little white lie to ease someone else's mind.

We deceive ourselves to better deceive others and we deceive others to gain survival advantage. In basketball, faking a flop is a common tactic to fool the referee into calling a foul on the other team. A batter decides to not swing on a 3-ball count. The pitch is on the edge of the plate, and the batter starts his motion toward first base knowing it might have been called a strike, but hoping to bias the umpire's decision. The catcher also tries to deceive the umpire by pulling his glove closer to the plate after catching it. They are all trying to deceive, and it's all part of the game.

Sometimes a little white lie or half truth can save a situation for others. Asked by Nazis whether Jews were being hidden in a house, the intentionally facetious answer made to appear like a joke "Yes they are under the table" was true but somewhat misleading. They were hiding under the floor, under the table.

We lie to ourselves to defend or enhance our image. We do this by placing blame on others when things go bad, and take responsibility when things go right. These biases show up in our life stories.

Stories are less convincing when luck is resorted to as an explanation. We are not satisfied with chance as a cause. Again, if we can get acceptable coherence without the use of luck, we will stay away from it as an explanation. If I did well in the stock market, does that mean I am a good investor? Could luck have anything to do with it? Chance will probably only come into our internal conversation briefly if at all. Admitting your success was due to luck is kind of like giving up on the pursuit of the cause. Luck is viewed as a humble modesty or as an out and out cop out.

Self-deception is risky in that it supports our thinking that we can do more physical and mental challenges than we really can. It's also risky if it becomes the rule rather than the exception. We can only call wolf just so many times before our deceptive behavior ceases to be effective, and should the deception be exposed, reputations can be forever lost.

In the courtroom a kind of unconscious self deception occurs when an eye witness is asked to pick a criminal from a simultaneous line-up. If there is not a 100% assurance on the part of the eye-witness, the question may subconsciously morph into who is *most likely* to be the criminal. The change in question makes it easier to pick an innocent person. Let's say you saw a man at the crime, and the line-up included all women and one man. The motivation to pick this man will surely be greater (even if he didn't look quite like the person seen at the crime) than if he had been present with other male suspects. This substituted question is probably easier to answer. Knowing that we were not sure of the identification beyond a reasonable doubt prompts us to build stories to support our decision. The more we think about it, the more truthful the answer appears to be to us, and the more confident we feel.

If our story includes deceit and self deception, we make the deception more robust by adopting new beliefs consistent with it and ignoring contradictory information. By the myside bias we deceive ourselves into thinking that we are so exceptional that the usual fair play rules are for the fools and do not apply to us. Studies have shown that when students are lead to believe they can cheat with impunity, they cheat more. This is one of the reasons that trust is so fragile; cheating often leads to personal benefit at a cost to others.

The house we live in or car we drive is often meant to send a message, a story, such as "I have resources." That message gets amplified with good clothes, or even verbal accent. Or we can say it with flowers, a lone flower saying, "I'm cheap." As previously mentioned, a story does not have to be true to be convincing. Pick up lines and tall tales may convince someone that you're special, notwithstanding the selfish deception at work. I once worked with an employee who must have had some kind of mental condition that promoted her constant lying. I was warned by others that she wasn't showing up when and where we thought she should. On the day after giving her counseling that she would be watched closely because I had to take into account rumors of her misbehavior, she changed her weekly report, after it had been approved. That was her last day. The point I am trying to make is that this was for me an exceptional case of deception because it was apparently part of her every day activities, part of her model of how to conduct herself. I'm sure her resumé would have been an interesting read in the realms of fiction.

"Although the biological approach defines 'advantage' in terms of survival and reproduction, the psychological approach often defines advantage as feeling better, or being happier. Self-deception occurs because we all want to feel good, and self-deception can help us do so."[287] What Trivers is talking about here is getting to that feel-good state of what Kahneman calls cognitive ease, which has been identified as a primary goal of our story telling. The motivation for 'getting there' can overwhelm our sense of doing things correctly, honestly. This is especially true if we know others are cheating to gain what those who didn't cheat are losing. To a deceiver, secretly taking the forbidden, illegal juice seems worth the home runs and the risk that goes with it. This deceit often includes self-deception, a practice that makes your deceit more believable to yourself and others. As George told Jerry on Seinfeld, "It's not a lie if you believe it." And you are more likely to believe it if it is repeated often enough.

Self-deception is, consistent with risk aversion, more strongly motivated by the possibility of loss than of gain.[288] We may dread being found out with the haunted conscience that follows, but sometimes we feel we cannot live with the losses that will occur if we don't deceive.

The fear of being found out enters our judgment when weighing the pros and cons of the choice between honesty and self-deception. Ariely wrote, "The link between creativity and dishonesty seems related to the ability to tell ourselves stories about how we are doing the right thing, even when we are not[289, 290]. The more creative we are, the more we are able to come up with convincing stories that help us justify our selfish interests." As Proust observed in Remembrance of Things Past, "It is not only by dint of

---

[287] Trivers pg 3
[288] Fang and Casadevall, "Why We Cheat", SciAm May / June 2013 ". . . dread is an even more powerful motivator than the desire for reward."
[289] Ariely pg 172
[290] ". . . neocortex size predicts the degree to which primates practice deception." Fang and Casadevall, SciAm Mind May/ June 2013

lying to others, but also of lying to ourselves, that we cease to notice that we are lying." A good liar doesn't know he is one.

If our stories aren't cohesive and coherent, we make up stuff, we lie, to make them at least appear to be so. This is part of the co-evolutionary battle between the deceiver and the deceived. Intelligence[291] is rewarded in the process of the deceiver coming up with new deceptions, while fighting to stay abreast of changes in the ability of those being deceived to detect them. Studies have shown that more intelligent species, as well as more creative children, are more likely to deceive than their peers.

Self-deception is sometimes detected as a companion to over-confidence.[292] Eye-witness's confidence in knowing the truth, as exposed in the Innocence Project, is often not justified. This is particularly true when deciding who is the criminal in a simultaneous lineup. Having made the choice, we may feel the need to back up that decision by creatively

---

[291] Trivers pg 5 "The evidence is clear and overwhelming that both the detection of deception and often its propagation have been major forces favoring the evolution of intelligence. It is perhaps ironic that dishonesty has often been the file against which intellectual tools for truth have been sharpened."

[292] CURRENT DIRECTIONS IN PSYCHOLOGICAL SCIENCE, VOLUME 11, NUMBER 5, OCTOBER 2002, The Confidence of Eyewitnesses in Their Identifications From Lineups, Gary L. Wells,et. Al. ". . . . confidence is governed by some factors that are unrelated to accuracy." "Confidence is not a reliable indicator of accuracy." Yet, confidence is a major factor that juries use to gauge the reliability they can have in an eye witness testimony. This is troubling due to the fact that innocents may be chosen from simultaneous lineups. A simultaneous lineup presents a group from which one is expected to be chosen to have been the person seen related to the crime. When asked to evaluate who was the person seen, the witnesses may unconsciously change the question to 'who is the most likely to have been that person'.

constructing narrative fallacies, that, if you are gullible enough (and we do want to believe), will ease any lingering doubts caused by the uncertainty of the decision. Our need to believe spills over into the stories we use to convince ourselves that we did right.

Self deception survives because it makes us feel good. ". . . an unjustifiably elevated belief in ourselves can increase our general well-being by helping us cope with stress; it can increase our persistence while doing difficult or tedious tasks; and it can get us to try new and different experiences."[293]

Stress

There are endless sources of stress. One important source of stress for our purposes is related to uncertainty and ambiguity. We find these conditions challenging, and so stressful. Many decisions are made without sufficient information to make you feel assured you went with the best one.[294] Rather than live with doubt, we make up a story to support our decisions. If that explanation has to include some untestable proposals (the devil made me do it) to put the mind at rest, we lower our standards of skepticism to accept the previously unacceptable. Our stories attempt to pull it all together as in the kite story or the Dude's carpet.[295] We can live with errors in these stories if they

---

[293] Ariely pg 158
[294] "Life is the art of drawing sufficient conclusions from insufficient premises." Samuel Butler
[295] Taleb Black pg 70 "To view the potency of narrative, consider the following statement "The king died and the queen died. Compare it to "The king died, and then the queen died of grief." ". . . . although we added information to the second statement, we effectively reduced the dimension of the total. The second sentence is, in a way, much lighter to carry

can enhance our fitness for survival and make us feel well. That they do this by being logical is not a requirement. "It is interesting to note that lacking control [stress] increases something called illusory pattern recognition. That is, when individuals are induced to feel a lack of control, they tend to see meaningful patterns in random data, as if responding to their unfortunate lack of control by generating (false) coherence in data that would then appear to give them greater control."[296] Under such conditions, we are more likely to find a way to squeeze the missing part into the puzzle and so ease our stress

A good story, one that's convincing, is one that leads to cognitive ease. Ideas link to each other without effort. There's no doubt or uncertainty. Here we can see a difference between the usual concept of a story where we do expect doubt and anxiety about who done it. Our use of story here is explanatory and as straightforward as possible. When System 1 is forming its interpretation, its story, it doesn't necessarily present the most rational one. It doesn't have time to judge amongst the rich realm of possibilities, that's what slow System 2 is for. If System 1 is receiving and transmitting that "All is OK", then System 2 is less bothered and may be freer but less motivated to analyze the S1 output.

"System 1 is not prone to doubt. It suppresses ambiguity and spontaneously constructs stories that are as coherent as possible." There is a bias to being certain because ". . . sustaining doubt is harder work than sliding into certainty.""System 1 runs ahead of the facts in constructing a rich image on the basis of scraps of evidence."". . . we are

---

and easier to remember; we now have one single piece of information in place of two. As we can remember it with less effort, we can also sell it to others, that is, market it better as a packaged idea. This, in a nutshell, is the definition and function of a narrative."

[296] Trivers pg 23

prone to exaggerate the consistency and coherence of what we see."[297]

"System 1 is designed to jump to conclusions from little evidence—and it is not designed to know the size of its jumps. Because of WYSIATI, only the evidence at hand counts. Due to confidence from coherence, the subjective confidence we have in our opinions reflects the coherence of the stories that System 1 and System 2 have worked on. The amount of evidence and its quality do not count for much, because poor evidence can make a very good story. For some of our most important beliefs we have no evidence at all, except that people we love and trust hold these beliefs. Considering how little we know, the confidence we have in our beliefs is preposterous—and it is also essential."[298]

When System 1 constructs a story, it doesn't consider what didn't happen. Its stories are anecdotes, not analyses. It doesn't harbor doubts like, 'Did you hear the story about the guy who didn't play racquet ball last week?' System 1 is not interested and does not know what *didn't* happen, again, a task for System 2. Neither is S2 so good at considering what didn't happen. Subsequently, our stories tend to exist without this important, hidden background; we don't tell since we didn't even think to ask for it.

System 1 is constantly working with a changing world and was favored by evolution to keep on dealing with the moment to moment. To facilitate this need for speed, System 1 relies on heuristics to form simplified interpretations of what it is sensing. As long as the story can at least achieve plausibility, System 1, for the moment, will be in its desired state of cognitive ease, satisfied, in the flow.

The essence of question substitution is that respondents offer a reasonable answer to a question that they have not been asked. Respondents who substitute one attribute for

---

[297]   K2011 pg 114
[298]   K2011 pg 209

another are not confused about the question that they are trying to answer—they simply fail to notice that they are answering a different one.[299] And when they do notice the discrepancy, they either modify the intuitive judgment or abandon it altogether.

This is why our answer to a question is often an answer to a different question leading us to make errors of the third kind, the correct answer to the wrong question.[300]) We seek coherency, explanation, patterns to reduce the discomfort, the stress of not knowing why, even if they lead us to a feeling of 'knowing' something that isn't true. It seems to me common among politicians, when asked an awkward question, begin their answer by giving some historical background or other comments that don't directly address the question. They get around the tough question by answering a question they are more comfortable with, an answer for which they have a model that indirectly touches on the question.

Emotions, such as fear, can quick start our responses to sound the alarm when time is of the essence. When in imminent danger, we can't wait for the rational S2 to finish its ponderings. It's go with your gut, time to make a call. When in doubt, play it safe, assume the worst. Shoot for a Type 1 error. Decision made, move on, play ball.

Another thing we do to get to cognitive ease is to insert bias (your model) into the process. For example, consider the System 1 reaction when you heard a rustle in the bushes. Is it a bear scavenging for a bite to eat? Might

---

[299] Everyman hears only what he understands. Goethe (we substitute questions in order to be able to answer them).

[300] In 1957, Allyn W. Kimball, a statistician with the Oak Ridge National Laboratory, proposed a different kind of error to stand beside "the first and second types of error in the theory of testing hypotheses". Kimball defined this new "error of the third kind" as being "the error committed by giving the right answer to the wrong problem"

it just be a sudden rise in the wind? Abruptly, your pleasant stroll has a new, uneasy feeling, cognitive stress if you will. Are you heading into danger? Are you just being paranoid? (Someone once told me paranoia is just a heightened sense of awareness). Your interpretation of your surroundings is no longer cohesive. There is a challenge to your expectations. Your amygdala is sparking before you're even aware that there is a possible threat. System 2 wakes up, focuses, and kicks into action. You're feeling the fear due to the hard choice to be made. Did you choose well? Are you feeling lucky today? Make a call, NOW! So, as best you can, you start analyzing the situation, coming to the realization that there are no bears in this neck of the woods, so you can relax.

Models as Stories

"Do not quench your inspiration and your imagination; do not become the slave of your model." Johann Wolfgang von Goethe . . . Your model is your story.

Models are those objects or mental pictures of how we think things are or ought to be. They serve to explain how something works or how things are expected to work. Each of us have models that are relevant to our life. When we speak of role models, it usually is in reference to someone we might want to pattern ourselves after such as our parents or perhaps a sport star like Roberto Clemente who lost his life serving others. An example of a physical model would be one that shows how the earth revolves around the sun. In general, models are ideals; they exist only in an ideal world. The behavior of gases is described by the *ideal* gas law. This equation allows us to make calculations of temperature, volume etc. that depend on the gas behaving as a perfectly ideal gas would. Since no gas is ideal, the calculated values from the 'law' are slightly off. Usually the difference between the real and the ideal are close enough for us mortals or they trigger the question of the cause for separation from the ideal.

Generally there is an explanatory story behind how the model came to be as it is and the model itself tells a story. The model shapes a story, and the story shapes the model. A paper plane could be a model for objects that fly. Tweeking the characteristics of our model plane shapes our knowledge of what changes improve the distance and straightness of its flight. As a young boy I used to amuse myself with taping tissues together that looked like a parachute and then tie a toy soldier to it to see how long it took before hitting the ground. I would race down from our 2nd floor apartment where I had dropped the chute to see if I could catch it before it hit the ground. I had a model of what would work and I played with the amount of tape, tissue, and toy weight to see what worked best. While looking for patterns we may find exceptions and contradictions that challenge the validity of our model. The mind is challenged to accommodate those uncomfortable facts that don't fit the model by finding a replacement to better address the discrepancies in the pattern.

While models would seem to work to our advantage, they can be overused in stories in an attempt to simplify. Here a few quotes that express this better than I can.

". . . we Platonify [model], liking known schemas and well-organized knowledge—to the point of blindness to reality. It is why we fall for the problem of induction, why we confirm."[301]

We do not describe the world we see, we see the world we can describe [models]. Rene Descartes

"Begin challenging your own assumptions [models]. Your assumptions are your windows on the world. Scrub them off every once in awhile, or the light won't come in."[302]

---

[301] Taleb Black pg 131
[302] Alan Alda

"The most erroneous stories are those we think we know best—and therefore never scrutinize or question." Stephen Jay Gould, paleontologist, biologist, author (1941-2002).

George Box: "All models are wrong, some are more useful."

To recap, we are born problem solvers and stories are one of the tools we use to ply that trade. Stories organize and integrate information in various forms: patterns, models, hypotheses, explanations etc. Good stories ease our minds. Simplicity, coherence, and anecdotes, all contribute to stories that feed this hedonistic goal of cognitive ease. Heuristics hasten the narrative. This may be useful and even necessary, but we need to be aware that we could be trading speed for loss of accuracy.

Some stories tie information together in a way that promotes understanding of the truth, others create only an illusion of understanding, superstition. Coherence in these stories is more important that content and we treat content as more important than reliability. Our tendency to gullibility biases us to believe what is presented to us and we tend not to think about missing information, and that can affect data reliability. Failure to detect lack of reliability in a story is due in part to our weaknesses for accepting small sample sizes, not taking into account base rates, and having memories that change over time to make a story become simpler and more cohesive, more ego friendly, familiar and accessible.

Biases that make us or our beliefs look good include selective memories, and behavior that seeks confirmation instead of disconfirmation. Not so comforting are stories that often allow randomness, good or bad luck, to be causal agents. Memories, central to the stories we recall, are reconstructed every time they are called upon. Some shards are lost along the way in order to allow new information to update the missing pieces of a story. How that updating is done can be an opportunity for unwarranted change.

Our emotions affect our decisions. At times they replace a question ('what's the best?') with an easier emotional response ('what do I like the best?). The Affect and other heuristics bias us to substitute a difficult question with an easier one.

"Narrative fallacies arise inevitably from our continuous attempt to make sense of the world. The explanatory stories that people find compelling are simple; are concrete rather than abstract; assign a larger role to talent, stupidity, and intentions than to luck; and focus on a few striking events that happened rather than on the countless events that failed to happen. Any recent salient event is a candidate to become the kernel of a causal narrative. Taleb suggests that we humans constantly fool ourselves by constructing flimsy accounts of the past and believing they are true."[303]

The Halo Effect contributes to a story's coherence. It also helps fill in the missing pieces of a story by adding congruent elements. This makes the story simpler and more easily remembered. The Halo Effect heuristic does this with plausible guesses that are consistent with what is already known. Having a consistent set of characteristics makes this story feel well known, and easily accessed. This heuristic is at work in the stereotypical assignment of consistent characteristics to a person for whom some other trait is well established. This kind of thinking seems consistent and plausible, and is often wrong. Since the Halo effect is all about consistency, it is a useful tool in making stories, a mental shortcut supporting story construction.

Overconfidence has a biasing influence on decision making. The diverse roots of overconfidence include myside bias, use of confirmatory evidence to pad opinions, a bias to believe, the Ikea effect, the lake Wobegon effect, simplification by data truncation, ease of not changing, ease of transition of acts to habit, neural processes that

---

[303] K2011 pg 199

physically change when support for current status erodes, superstitions, memory reconstructions, self-deception, participation with group think, unsupported detection and belief in patterns, inappropriate reliance on intuition, and trust in anecdotal accounts over statistical explanations. Overconfidence and hubristic pride are major reasons for not changing our stories when we should.

Last Words, closing time

We make better decisions when we can integrate our subconscious with the conscious. While the subconscious works unrecognized in the background, we can influence it in the direction of our choice. We can be aware of how to use priming to put ourselves or others in a desired frame of mind. Our questions can be re-structured to purposely bias our answers. While we might not be interested in using the heuristics in this book to influence others, they may be used, purposefully or not, by others to influence us. Our awareness of this possibility may be enough to avoid making biased decisions that are not to our benefit.

Studies have shown that one of the best ways to avoid the influence of these cognitive illusions is to slow down. Problems that appear simple and easily answered are often not. It takes a little extra work to look for the hidden. As physicists like to remind us, everything is connected to everything. This seems as true for our brains as for the stars above. Eighty six billion neurons with a trillion synapses are enough to provide endless options for finding new ways to sense, judge, and decide what, if anything, we ought to be doing. We can expect less speculation and more understanding of how our minds make decisions as we continue to be mindful enough to discover what it is that we don't know.

Appendix One

The following is from Piattelli-Palmaarine Palmarini Pg 83

"Here is the so-called juror's fallacy. You are a member of a jury. A taxi driver is accused of having run down a pedestrian on a stormy night and having fled the scene of the accident. The prosecutor, in asking for a conviction, bases his whole case on a single witness, a lady who saw the accident from her window a little way away. The lady testifies that she saw the pedestrian struck by a blue taxi and then saw the taxi drive away from the scene of the accident. The accused works for a taxi company whose taxis are al blue. During the trial, the following emerges:

1   There are only two taxi companies in this town. The whole fleet of one company is green; the other has only blue cabs. Eighty-five percent of all the taxis on the road that night were green, and only 15 percent were blue.

2   The single witness has under gone a number of vision tests in conditions similar to those on the night of the accident. She has been shown to be

able to distinguish a blue taxi from a green one 80 percent o the time.

On the basis of the sworn testimony of the witness, and the data offered in 1 and 2, what is the probability the taxi really was blue?

The following is from http://plus.maths.org/content/solution-taxi-problem-revisited

Let's write down the information that we are given using probability statements. First, we need to introduce some notation. When we write $P(A|B)$ we mean: the probability of event A *given that* (denoted by "|") the event B has occurred.

For the taxi problem we have

$$P(\text{witness says that the taxi is blue}|\text{taxi is blue})$$
$$= P(\text{witness is correct}) = 0.8;$$

this probability statement tells the police how *likely* the witness is to be correct about the taxi being blue. We are also told that $P(\text{taxi is blue}) = 0.85$; this probability statement describes the strength of belief that the police have in the hypothesis that the taxi is blue *prior* to the witness coming forward.

What really interests the police is

$$P(\text{taxi is blue}|\text{witness says that the taxi is blue}).$$

In other words, they want to know the probability that a blue taxi is involved in the crime given the data that they have from the witness. Bayes' theorem provides us with a way of finding this probability from the two known probabilities:

$P(\text{witness says that the taxi is blue}|\text{taxi is blue})$ and $P(\text{taxi is blue}).$

In its simplest form Bayes' theorem can be written as:

$$P(A|B) = \{P(B|A)P(A)\} / P(B) = \{0.8 \times 0.85\} / 0.71 = 0.68 / 0.71 = 0.96$$

for two events A and B, provided $P(B) > 0$.
The denominator $P(B)$ can be calculated from the formula:

$$P(B) = P(B|A)P(A) + P(B|\text{not } A)\, P(\text{not } A)$$

If you haven't met these formulae before, please don't worry. Just take them on trust. If you want to learn more about them, have a look at a book such as the one mentioned at the bottom of the page.

It is worth noting that Bayes' theorem allows us to reverse conditional probabilities: if we know $P(A)$ and $P(B)$, we can find $P(A|B)$ from $P(B|A)$ (and $P(B|A)$ from $P(A|B)$ as well).

To apply Bayes' theorem to the taxi problem let A be the event that the taxi is blue and B be the event that the witness says that the taxi is blue. We already know that $P(B|A) = 0.8$ and $P(A) = 0.85$. It is easy to work out $P(B|\text{not } A)$ and $P(\text{not } A)$:

$P(B|\text{not } A)$

= P(witness says that the taxi is blue|taxi is not blue)
= P(witness is not correct)
= 1—P(witness is correct)
= 1—0.8
= 0.2

$P(\text{not } A)$

= P(taxi is not blue)
= 1—P(taxi is blue)
= 1—0.85
= 0.15

(It happens in this case that $P(B|\text{not } A) = 1 - P(B|A)$; please note, however, that this result is **not** generally true.)

We can now calculate $P(B)$:

$P(B)$

$= P(B|A)P(A) + P(B|\text{not } A)P(\text{not } A)$
$= (0.8 \times 0.85) + (0.2 \times 0.15)$
$= 0.71$

Hence, P(blue taxi is involved|witness says that the taxi is blue)

$P(A|B) = \{P(B|A)P(A)\} \, / \, P(B) = \{0.8 \times 0.85\}$
$/ 0.71 = 0.68 \, / \, 0.71 = 0.96$

which is exactly the result given in the solution to the taxi problem by the contingency table approach.

The following is from http://plus.maths.org/content/os/issue2/puzzle/taxisolution

We know that 85% of the taxis in Carborough are blue, the other 15% of taxis being green.

Suppose that there's no bias for any particular blue or green taxi to be involved in such incidents. Then consider 100 possible cases (contingencies), in which taxis are involved, in proportion to their numbers. Each case is equally probable. We expect 85 cases to involve blue taxis, 15 to involve green. If a blue taxi were really involved, the witness might report blue (with 80% probability) or green (with 20% probability). If a green taxi were really involved, the witness might report blue (with 20% probability) or green (with 80% probability). The number of times that these outcomes are expected to occur in each of these four cases are shown in the table below. (Tables like this are called contingency tables.)

So, given that the witness reported seeing a blue taxi, we must use the row in the table corresponding to the reported blue taxi. We have 68+3 = 71 equally likely cases and the probability that a blue taxi really was involved is 68/71 = 96%.

A more interesting and surprising result is obtained in the case when the witness reports a green taxi. Many people on being asked this problem will say that if the witness reports a green taxi, then there is an 80% probability that a green taxi was involved. This however is incorrect, as the following argument shows. The contingency table is the same as above but now we must use the row in the table corresponding to the reported green taxi. We have 17+12 = 29 equally likely cases and the probability that a green taxi really was involved is 12/29 = 41%. The cases of correct identification of green are swamped by the false identifications of blue, and the witness's evidence is of no practical value.

There are two key probabilities in the above formulation. The first is P(witness says that the taxi is blue|taxi is blue). Since the only *data* available to the police is the account given by the witness, we may think of this probability as P(data|taxi is blue). This probability is known as the *likelihood* of the data given the hypothesis that the taxi is blue, and represents how likely the data are if the taxi is blue.

The second key probability is P(taxi is blue). This probability is known as the *prior* probability that the taxi is blue, and represents the strength of belief that the police give to the taxi being blue before they learn of the data. We have seen that Bayes' theorem enables us to find P(taxi is blue|data) from the likelihood and the prior probability. The probability P(taxi is blue|data) is known as the *posterior* probability that the taxi is blue because it is the probability that the taxi is blue *after* the data have been taken into account.

It is now simple to work out P(taxi is not blue|witness says the taxi is blue)

P(taxi is not blue|witness says that the taxi is blue)

$= P(\text{not } A|B)$
$= 1 - P(A|B)$
$= 1 - 0.96$
$= 0.04$

The probability P(taxi is blue|witness says that the taxi is blue) is very much larger than P(taxi is not blue|witness says that the taxi is blue). Accordingly, if the witness says that the taxi is blue, the police should conclude that it is indeed blue.

Up to now we have considered the case when the data available is the statement of the witness that the taxi is blue. In the solution to the taxi problem the other case when the witness says that the taxi is not blue is also considered. It was found that:

P(taxi is blue|witness says that the taxi is not blue) = 0.59

and that

P(taxi is not blue|witness says that the taxi is not blue) = 0.41

The probability P(taxi is not blue|witness says that the taxi is not blue) turns out to be smaller than P(taxi is blue|witness says that the taxi is not blue). This means that, even though the witness says that the taxi is not blue, the police should conclude that the taxi is blue. Here the prior belief of the police about the color of the taxi has swamped the data supplied by the witness. In both the above cases the police estimate the color of the taxi as the one (between blue and not blue) that maximizes the posterior probability.

Appendix Two

BIRTHDAY PROBLEMS

How many randomly chosen people are enough to make the chance of their sharing a birthday 50%?

Sometimes probability questions like this are more easily solved by changing the question to how many randomly chosen people are enough to assure they don't have the same birthday. Once we have that number, that is, the probability of not sharing a birthday, we can simply subtract it from "1" to give the answer to the chance of sharing a birthday.

To start, what is the probability of two people not sharing a birthday? In a 366 day year, there are 365 ways not to share. That is, there is a 365/366 (99.73%) chance of not sharing. When we change the question to what is the probability of three people not sharing a birthday? Since there are 364 ways remaining that do not match, the answer is [(365x366) x (364x366)] that is, 99.18%. Continue adding people to the equation in this way until you reach the number of people required for a 49% probability of not sharing a birthday. That occurs at 23.

A variant of this problem asks, given a specific date, how many people must there be to make a match with a specific date, such as mine or the 4th of July. For one person, the chance of matching a particular date is 365/366. For any person, the chance of not matching a particular date is 365/366. The probability of two people not matching is 365/366 x 365/366, or $(365/366)^2$. Continue this progression until the calculation gives close to 50% which happens at about 254 people.

Birthday Paradox. (AVAILABILITY) see pg 20 K&T. This is not a paradox in the sense of leading to a logical contradiction, but is called a paradox because the mathematical truth contradicts naïve intuition: most people estimate that the chance of two individuals sharing the same birthday in a group of 23 is much lower than 50%.

Three sisters give birth on the same day.
Chance Magazine, Spring 2001, pp 23-25
Nathan Wetzel

On March 14 the Stevens Point Journal asked: What is the probability that three sisters would give birth on the same day? This event happened when sisters Karralee Morgan, Marrianne Asay and Jennifer Hone all gave birth on March 11, 1998 in American Fork Utah. The Stevens Point Journal article included the comment:

If the three mothers hadn't all gotten pregnant about the same time, then you could say that each baby had a one-in-365 chance of having March 11 as his or her birthday. The probability of the occurrence of the three successive births on the same date would be about one in 50 million. (or $(1/365)^3$)

We have often been asked questions about coincidences like this and have never felt very comfortable about our answers. Wetzel shows us why this might be by considering five different versions of this problem and indicating how we might estimate the odds for each of the five. Here are his five versions with his estimates:

1. Given three particular sisters who each will give birth to a baby this year, what is the probability that they will all give birth on March 11? Ans. $(1/365)^3$ or about 1 in 50 million

2. Given three particular sisters who each will give birth to a baby this year, what is the probability they will all give birth on the same day? Ans. $365/365^3$ or 1 in 133,225

3. Before they had their babies, what was the probability that the three sisters referenced in the Stevens Point Journal newspaper article would give birth on March 11?
   Ans. about 1 in 500,000

4. Before they had their babies, what was the probability that the three sisters referenced in the Stevens Point Journal newspaper article would all give birth on the same day? Ans. about 1 in 6,000

5. What is the probability that somewhere in the United States there will be three sisters who all give birth on the same day sometime during the next year? Ans. lower bound; about 1 in 407

Wetzel remarks: The last question is the closest to what we believe people mean when they ask the question "What is the probability that the three sisters would give birth on the same day?" It is also the hardest to estimate since you have to estimate the number of families in which there are three sisters all of childbearing age and all becoming pregnant this year.

Appendix Three

THE (PETER) WASON CARD
SELECTION TASK

The Wason card selection task is a problem often used to focus on our decision making processes. Our tendency to search for confirmatory evidence tends to lead us to some incorrect decisions in this task. The following are related example problems of how we are generally biased to look for confirmation when we should be challenging a belief with a search for disconfirmation.

From Kida, pg 163/4

To determine if a hypothesis is likely to be true, we should try to prove it false. Why? It's impossible to prove a hypothesis is correct with certainty, but we can disprove it with one observation. And so, disconfirming evidence can be very useful in our decision making.

Below are four cards. Each card has a letter on one side and a number on the other. Two of the cards are letter-side up, and two of the cards are number-side up. The rule to be tested is this: For these four cards, if a card has a vowel on its letter side, it has an even number on its number side. Your task is to decide which card or cards must be turned over to find out whether the rule is true or false.

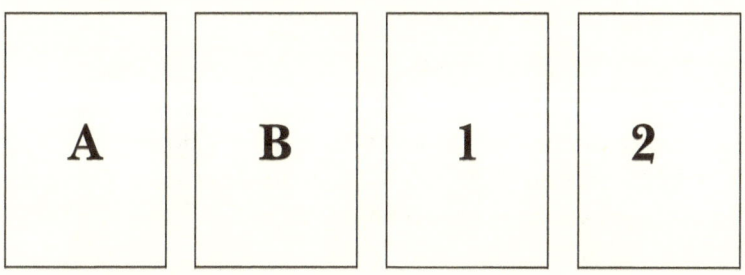

Most people understand the value of vowel **A**: it can confirm with an even number and disconfirm if an odd number is on the other side. In contrast, the consonant **B** tells us nothing. Consonants can have either odd or even numbers neither of which confirm nor disconfirm the rule. If the card **2** has an associated vowel, we could say that it is consistent with (confirms) the rule. If it has a consonant which is outside of the rules, there is no use here for this card. The **1** card could disconfirm the rule if it has a vowel, since all vowels must have an even number on their other sides. If **1** has a consonant it neither confirms nor disconfirms the rule. Card 1 would be sufficient to disprove the rule

To sum up, either A or 1 could disprove or confirm the rule. If the first one chosen is A, and it is found to confirm the rule, 1 is needed since it could disconfirm, and vice versa.

"Most people get the answer wrong, and it has been difficult to figure out why. About half of them say you should pick A and 2: a vowel to see if there is an even number on its reverse side and an even number to see if there is a vowel on its reverse. We are more likely to look for confirmation than disconfirmation. We can more efficiently come to a decision by looking for disconfirmation. Once we have found that, no amount of confirmation will be sufficient to overcome that fact that the rule is not always true." From Scientific American November/December 2009 Rational and Irrational Thought: The Thinking That IQ Tests Miss. Keith E. Stanovich.

Here's another similar, more realistic situation. The structure of the task in logical terms are underlined.

David planted a garden with colorful flowers. He has not been able to enjoy it, though, because deer from the forest nearby have been nibbling on them.

He would like to keep the deer out of his garden. His grandmother said that in the old days, she kept deer away by spraying them with an herbal tea—lacana—in her garden. The rule to be tested was:

"If you spray lacana tea on your flowers, deer will stay out of your yard."
"If P happens, then Q happens"

This sounded dubious. So David convinced some of his neighbors to spray their flowers with lacana tea, to see what would happen. You are interested in seeing whether any of the results of this experiment violate Grandma's rule.

The cards below represent four yards near David's house. Each card represents one yard. One side of the card tells whether or not lacana tea was sprayed on the flowers in a yard, and the other side tells whether or not deer stayed out of that yard.

Which of the following cards would you definitely need to turn over to see if what happened in any of these yards violated Grandma's rule:

"If you spray lacana tea on your flowers, deer will stay out of your yard."

Don't turn over any more cards than are absolutely necessary.

The logically correct answer is:
***P** = sprayed with lacana tea and **not-Q** = deer did not stay away*

Here's a version of the task from
From Gigerenzer Rationality pg 12:

"If a previous employee gets a pension from the firm, and that person must have worked for the firm for at least 10 years." This is the rule we asked to test.

got a pension	worked 10 years for the firm	did not get a pension	worked 8 years for the firm

The four cards read: got a pension, worked 10 years for the firm, did not get a pension, worked 8 years for the firm. One group of *participants was put in the role of the employer* and asked to check those cards (representing files of pervious employees) that could reveal whether the rule was violated. The far majority picked "got a pension" and "worked for 8 years." Note that this choice is consistent with both the laws of the truth table and the goal of *cheater detection.* Proponents of content-blind norms interpreted this and similar results as indicating that social contracts somehow facilitate logical reasoning. But when we cued the participants in the role of an employee, the far majority picked "did not get a pension" and "worked for 10 years."(In contrast, in the employer's group, no participant had checked this information.) Now the result was inconsistent with the truth table, but from the employee's perspective, again consistent with the goal of not being cheated. Search for information was Machiavellian: to avoid being cheated oneself, not to avoid cheating others."

The following is from Eagleman Incognito pg 85-86

The card task is analogous to a bouncer at a bar who must throw out underage drinkers. He's confronted with four people: a beer drinker, a cola drinker, a 28-year-old, and a 16-year-old.

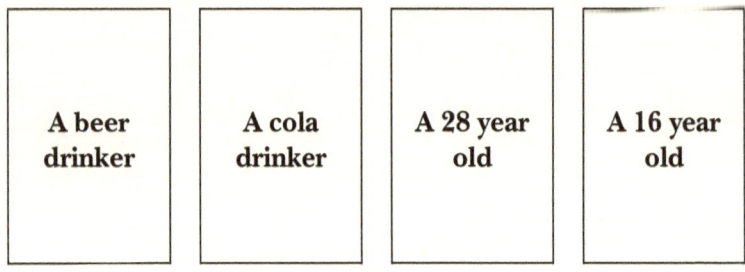

Which two should he interrogate (flip card) further? The rule to be tested is that no under-aged individual is drinking alcohol. Here it's clear that it is the beer drinker and 16-year-old who must be interrogated.

Appendix Four

Monty Hall Problem, another veridical paradox.

A *veridical paradox* produces a result that appears absurd (counterintuitive) but is demonstrated to be true nevertheless.

The Monty Hall Problem is named after the host of a TV program named Let's Make a Deal which aired from 1963 to 1990.

In this game show you are given the opportunity to select one closed door of three, behind one of which there is a prize. The other two doors hide "goats" (or some other such "non-prize"), or nothing at all. Once you have made your selection, Monty Hall will open one of the remaining two doors, revealing that it does *not* contain the prize. He then asks you if you would like to switch your selection to the other unopened door, or stay with your original choice. Here is the problem: Does it matter if you switch?

This problem had existed in various forms before being referred to Marilyn vos Savant who had a regular column in the Parade magazine. She used her column to solve problems and puzzles. Once upon a time she was listed in the Guinness Book of World Records under highest IQ.

Her answer, that one should always switch in this game, was met with some incredibly arrogant communications. Four examples:

"You blew it, and you blew it big! Since you seem to have difficulty grasping the basic principle at work here, I'll explain. After the host reveals a goat, you now have a one-in-two chance of being correct. Whether you change your selection or not, the odds are the same. There is enough mathematical illiteracy in this country, and we don't need the world's highest IQ propagating more. Shame!"

"I have been a faithful reader of your column, and I have not, until now, had any reason to doubt you. However, in this matter (for which I do have expertise), your answer is clearly at odds with the truth."

"May I suggest that you obtain and refer to a standard textbook on probability before you try to answer a question of this type again?"

"You are utterly incorrect about the game show question, and I hope this controversy will call some public attention to the serious national crisis in mathematical education. If you can admit your error, you will have contributed constructively towards the solution of a deplorable situation. How many irate mathematicians are needed to get you to change your mind?"

Case	Original door choice	Probability	Don't Switch Outcome	Switch Outcome	Don't Switch EV	Switch EV
1	Right	1/3	Win	Lose	1/3	0
2	Wrong	2/3	Lose	Win	0	2/3
Total		1			1/3	2/3

"EV" refers to "expected value."

Case 1

If you always stay (do not change) you will win 33% of the time

Can you do better by switching?

In those cases where you didn't chose a winner, that is, 2/3 of the time, if you always call switch, the first door with no prize (by definition you did not chose this prizeless door) is no longer a choice. There would remain two doors, one of which (with no prize) would be eliminated by Monty. That leaves you with the door with the prize 100% of the time for the 2/3 of the times that your first choice (door #1) was empty and you switched. If you always choose door #1, you will win 1/3 of the time. If you decide to always switch after Monty eliminates one, you will have door 1 which in the 2/3 situation is by definition a loser, and one final door which is always a winner for 2/3 of the time.

By always switching, you will win 67% (2/3) of the time.

Okay, say you did select the *correct* door initially. How often will this happen? One time out of three: $1/3$. In that case, both of the two remaining doors will be "losers", and Monty Hall will open one of them leaving your correct door and the remaining incorrect door. So, if you switch, you'll switch to the wrong door since you picked the right one to begin with. Since you will be right one-third of the time, that means that if you stay with your first choice, you'll get the prize one-third of the time. That's what happens when your initial choice is correct. So we know that the best you can do by staying is to get the prize $1/3$ of the time.

Now let's look at the other possibility: that your initial choice is *incorrect*. Only one time out of three is your first choice going to be correct. That means that the remaining times, your initial choice is going to be the wrong door. You're going to choose the wrong door $2/3$ of the time.

That means that $2/3$ of the time, the other two doors (taken together) hide the prize.

This leaves your initial choice, which is incorrect; and the remaining door, which hides the prize. We've already determined that your initial choice will be incorrect $2/3$ of the time (it is those times we are looking at here). We've shown how that means (if it needed to be explained at all) that $2/3$ of the time, the prize will be behind one of those two other doors. But in showing you which of those two doors does not hide the prize, Monty Hall has told you which does: the only one left. Keep thinking of the two doors, in aggregate, as having a $2/3$ probability of hiding the prize. Now imagine that you know (and you do) which of the two doesn't. You can still think of the probabilities in aggregate—$2/3$—but now eliminate one possible choice. You might say that the remaining door "inherits" the probability of the eliminated door—so now for that one door, the probability of it being the door which hides the prize is $2/3$. Your initial choice has only one chance in three of being right—this remaining door has two chances in three. Should you switch? Hmm.

The Wrong "Solution", and a More Concise Explanation of the Correct Solution.

I didn't discuss what the general, incorrect, intuitive "solution" to this problem is: I didn't want to mislead, or confuse you. It was, in fact, my own initial response to this problem. In short, I felt that after Monty showed me a losing door that left two: one is right, the other wrong. It seemed to me, and to most people, that it's a $50/50$ proposition: it doesn't matter if you switch, or not. Further, just to test my instinct, I asked myself "Well, did Monty Hall reveal any information in opening the losing door?" And it seemed to me that he did not. *But he did.*

He did, because he *always has to open a losing door:* one losing door is always eliminated. The probabilities of your initial choice being correct and the remaining choices have to sum to equal one. Therefore, the probability of the remaining choices has to sum to equal one minus the probability of your initial choice. In this case (with three doors), they have to sum to equal $2/3$. Say a door isn't opened. Then, you would have two to switch to (if you choose to switch—this would be like "changing your mind"), and your chance of picking the correct door would be $1/2 \times 2/3$. Well, that's $1/3$, just like your initial choice. But if Monty has to open a door, then you'll only have one door to switch to. In this case (which is the Monty Hall problem), you'll pick the remaining door—so that'd be $1 \times 2/3$. And that's a probability of $2/3$.

- Case 1: You've picked the right door to start with. If you switch, you'll lose.
- Case 2: You've picked the wrong door to start with. The host shows you the other wrong door, so if you switch, you'll clearly win.

Now, Case 1 only happens $1/3$ of the time, and Case 2 happens $2/3$ of the time. Therefore, if you follow the strategy of always switching, you'll win $2/3$ of the time. Whereas, if you never switch, you'll of course get the right door only $1/3$ of the time. If that's not clear enough, take a look at the following table. "EV" refers to "expected value."

Case	Original door choice	Probability	Don't Switch Outcome	Switch Outcome	Don't Switch EV	Switch EV
1	Right	1/3	Win	Lose	1/3	0
2	Wrong	2/3	Lose	Win	0	2/3
Total		1			1/3	2/3

Appendix Five

HOW TO MEASURE THE HEIGHT OF
A BUILDING WITH A BAROMETER

As an example looking at a problem from different perspectives, the apocryphal story of how to use a barometer to measure the height of a building.

Some time ago I received a call from a colleague who asked if I would be the referee on the grading of an examination question. He was about to give a student a zero for his answer to a physics question, while the student claimed he should receive a perfect score and would if the system were not set up against the student. The instructor and the student agreed to submit this to an impartial arbiter, and I was selected.

I went to my colleague's office and read the examination question, "Show how it is possible to determine the height of a tall building with the aid of a barometer."

The student had answered, "Take a barometer to the top of the building, attach a long rope to it, lower the barometer to the street and then bring it up, measuring the length of the rope. The length of the rope is the height of the building."

I pointed out that the student really had a strong case for full credit since he had answered the question completely and correctly. On the other hand, if full credit was given, it could well contribute to a high grade for the student in his physics course. A high grade is supposed to certify competence in physics, but the answer did not confirm this. I suggested that the student have another try at answering the question. I was not surprised that my colleague agreed, but I was surprised that the student did.

I gave the student six minutes to answer the question with the warning that the answer should show some knowledge of physics. At the end of five minutes, he had not written anything. I asked if he wished to give up, but he said no. He had many answers to this problem; he was just thinking of the best one. I excused myself for interrupting him and asked him to please go on. In the next minute he dashed off his answer which read, "Take the barometer to the top of the building and lean over the edge of the roof. Drop that barometer, timing its fall with a stopwatch. Then using the formula $S = \frac{1}{2}at^2$, calculate the height of the building."

At this point I asked my colleague if he would give up. He conceded, and I gave the student almost full credit.

In leaving my colleague's office, I recalled that the student had said he had many other answers to the problem, so I asked him what they were. "Oh yes," said the student. "There are a great many ways of getting the height of a tall building with a barometer. For example, you could take the barometer out on a sunny day and measure the height of the barometer and the length of its shadow, and the length of the shadow of the building and by the use of a simple proportion, determine the height of the building."

"Fine," I asked. "And the others?"

"Yes," said the student." There is a very basic measurement method that you will like. In this method you take the barometer and begin to walk up the stairs. As you climb the stairs, you mark off the length of the barometer along the wall. You then count the number of marks, and this will give you the height of the building in barometer units. A very direct method."

"Of course, if you want a more sophisticated method, you can tie the barometer to the end of a string, swing it as a pendulum, and determine the value of 'g' at the street level and at the top of the building. From the difference of the two values of 'g' the height of the building can be calculated."

Finally, he concluded, there are many other ways of solving the problem. "Probably the best," he said, "is to take the barometer to the basement and knock on the superintendent's door. When the superintendent answers, you speak to him as follows, 'Mr. Superintendent, here I have a fine barometer. If you tell me the height of this building, I will give you this barometer.'"

At this point I asked the student if he really did know the conventional answer to this question. He admitted that he did, said that he was fed up with high school and college instructors trying to teach him how to think, using the "scientific method"

Appendix Six

DIAGNOSTICS

The following lesson is that while some questions appear to be equivalent, (see inversion confusion, chapter 3) when they are not. Another lesson is that the relative ease of using actual counts vs. percentages simplifies the analysis, and so supports the thinking that our intuitions do not work well with probabilities. Taleb The Black Swan pg 133: ". . . probability, the mother of all abstract notions." Gigerenzer Calculated Risks pg 37: "Why is it so difficult for even highly educated people to make inferences on the basis of probabilities? The fact that the notion of mathematical probability developed so late—later than most key philosophical concepts has been called the "scandal of philosophy"

Compare the following two queries.

"A" IS THE PROBABILITY THAT A PERSON HAS A CONDITION GIVEN THAT THEY HAVE A POSITIVE TEST.

VS

"B" IS THE PROBABILITY THAT A PERSON HAS A POSITIVE TEST GIVEN THAT THEY HAVE THE CONDITION.

Are they the same?

0.1% in population of interest has the condition

90% with the condition test positive.

5% without the condition test positive

For 10,000 people, 100 have the condition, of which 90 test positive

For the 9,900 that don't have the condition, 495 will test positive.

FOR A, $= 90/(90 + 495) = 19\%$

FOR B, $= 90\%$

This error of inversion confusion occurs in the medical field when, for example, it is known that 90% of patients with the condition will test positive, so it is expected that a positive test means about a 90% chance of having the disease. As can be seen by the above calculations, this is a false assumption.

The following is from Gigerenzer, Calculated Risks pg 41-42: "Imagine that you conduct breast cancer screening using mammography in a particular region of the country. The following information is available about asymptomatic women aged 40 to 50 in such regions who participate in mammography screening: The probability that one of these women has breast cancer is 0.8 percent. If a woman has breast cancer, the probability is 90 percent that she will have a positive mammogram. If a woman does not have breast cancer, the probability is 7 percent and that she will still have a positive mammogram. Imagine a woman who has a positive mammogram.

What is the probability that she actually has breast cancer?"

This question is often posed to expose the difficulty of thinking in a way that gets the right results. It seems easiest to focus on the upper left quadrant of the table (see below) that lays out this information is a supportive fashion using natural frequencies (counts)

The question is repeated, exchanging counts ('natural frequencies') for percentages.

Eight out of every 1,000 woman have breast cancer. Of these 10 women with breast cancer, 7 will have a positive mammogram. Of the remaining 990 women who don't have breast cancer, some 70 will still have a positive mammogram. Imagine a sample of women who have positive mammograms in screening. How many of these women actually have breast cancer?

The Contingency table: Given 8 per 1000 have breast cancer:

Test result	Has cancer (8)	Does not have cancer (992)
positive	7 = (0.9*8) = 0.72	65 = 7% * 992
negative	1 = (0.1*8) = 0.08	857 = 93% (922)
	8 = 7.2 + 0.8	922 = 65 + 857

Notice how much easier it is now is to think about this question. Seven women have breast cancer, and another 70 test positive (falsely) for cancer. Given a positive test for cancer (70 + 7), what is the probability that the person actually has the disease? In other words what is the probability that a specific outcome divided by all possible outcomes?

Glossary

Every word was once a poem.
Ralph Waldo Emerson, writer and philosopher
(1803-1882)

A

Anchoring and Adjustment is a heuristic that works by being exposed to a random number prior to being asked to estimate a number. The Anchor provides a point from which we adjust. Write down the last 2 numbers of your Social Security prior to being asked the number of countries in Africa. If your 2 numbers are relatively high, your estimate is also likely to be relatively high.

Anchoring effects are somewhat different for System 1 (automatic priming) and System 2 (a deliberate process of adjustment). (K2011pg120)

The Availability Heuristic influences our estimates by substituting the question of how frequently an event occurs to the question of how accessible the answer is. If you are constantly worrying about the safety of your next flight, you may overestimate the probability with which a bad trip will happen.

Associative Learning. This is a "learning" or "conditioning" term that refers to learning that two different events occur or happen together. This is really a fundamental component of conditioning since a response to a stimulus won't really be learned if the organism doesn't get the point that the stimulus and response are supposed to occur together. This doesn't have to be a conscious learning but the association must be made for the learning to occur. For example, will a rat learn to press a lever if it never makes the association between pressing the lever and getting the reward? Or why would a dog salivate to a bell if it never makes the connection between the bell and getting food?   http://www.alleydog.com/glossary/definition. php?term=Associative%20Learning

Affect Heuristic see page 140 of K2011, substitutions, as related to benefits and risk, is like a halo effect that when benefits were considered high, risk tracked low. There isn't necessarily any link between the two, but for our feelings to be consistent, if we feel good about, say, a given technology, then for consistency's sake, the positiveness does link one with the other.

Associative memory is associated with S1

B

Bear in the Bush I use this scenario to represent the basic kinds of errors we can commit and what the relative consequences of being wrong can be. The bear in a bush problem, as is the case in many decision making scenarios, presents two kinds of errors, named Type 1 and Type 2. Type 1 error occurs when you think there is a bear in the bush but there isn't, and Type 2 error occurs when you don't think there is a bear, but there is.

Base rates are those probabilities that describe the rate of occurrence of instances of a condition in the relevant population.

C

Cognitive dissonance is the uncomfortable feeling you get when there is a conflict between the judgment of need for change and a contrary prior feeling or belief.

Cherry Picking (confirmation bias) Taleb Black pg 55, "By a mental mechanism I call naïve empiricism, we have a natural tendency to look for instances that confirm and our story and our vision of the world—these instances are always easy to find." Cherry picking involves choosing the results that you like that support your position.

Consensus bias occurs when we incorrectly think that everyone thinks as you do.

Repeated words elicit the sense of familiarity. After being exposed to certain words, their appearance in the future is more quickly recognized than words that were not shown in the experiment. This quick recognition gives the feeling of familiarity resulting in *Cognitive ease.*

Cognitive ease K2011 pg 67 "The link between positive emotion and cognitive ease in System 1 has a long evolutionary history."

(CE) Cognitive ease K2011 pg 105 System 1 "Links a sense of cognitive ease to illusions of truth, pleasant feelings, and reduced vigilance."

Cognitive ease is associated with words such as comfortable, familiarity, the feeling of knowing, trust, coherent/cohesive, happy, bright primary colors, readable font, predictable, positive, etc. Cognitive Ease is enhanced by repetition, rhyming, lack of contradictions, supporting information.

K2011 pg 69 "*Cognitive ease* is both a cause and a consequence of a pleasant feeling." It is often associated with overconfidence.

K2011 pg 60 *Cognitive ease* is supported by feelings of familiarity, trust, trueness, goodness, attributed to repetition, good mood, clarity and understanding, and primed ideas.

Cognitive strain K2011 pg 59 "Strained indicates that a problem exists, which will require increased mobilization of System 2."

Conjunction fallacy Multiple specific conditions are judged more probable than a single general one. Small red balloons are more probable than red balloons.

Cohesiveness and Coherency lend credence to a story.

> To make a passage *cohesive*, start sentences with information the reader is already familiar with. This works best when the last few words of each sentence set up information that appears in the first few words of the next.

> To make a passage *coherent,* ensure that each
> sentence deals with the same topic and include
> a sentence that states what the whole passage
> supports or explains. http://cseweb.ucsd.
> edu/~ztatlock/blog/cohesive-vs-coherent/

Confidence intervals. These are, generally speaking, limits
within which our estimation of a number lies with a given
probability. See Natrella for a good discussion.

The *Congruence bias* states that we tend to look for
confirmation more frequently than *disconfirmation.* Looking
for confirmation keeps getting supporting information. See
the 4-card problem in Appendix 3.

Counter Intuitive It's not what you think it is.

Confirmation bias is the tendency to choose information that
is supportive of our beliefs and to ignore non-confirming
information.

D

Declarative memory is associated with S2

Disconfirmation. The search for results that challenge the
correctness of a theory or hypothesis

E

Emotions. (Burton pg 36) "Psychologists commonly divide
certain feeling states into primary emotions, such as
happiness, sadness, fear, anger, surprise, and disgust and

secondary or social emotions, such as embarrassment, jealousy, guilt, and pride."

The Endowment effect can be summarized as the bias you have to stay with your current beliefs and material things and unless you are paid more to sell them than it cost you to obtain them.

Explicit knowledge see tacit knowledge.

F

Shermer pg 268 "How beliefs are framed often determines how they are assessed, and this is called the *framing effect*, or the tendency to draw different conclusions based on how data are presented."

Fast and Frugal—see Gigerenzer, Mortals pg 7: "A heuristic is fast if it can solve a problem in little time and frugal if it can solve it with little information."

FEMA Failure Effect Mode Analysis A procedure for the analysis of potential failure modes based on likelihood, severity, and ability to detect. Values used for these analyses are seldom completely free of subjectivity. As per a conversation with Ron Kenett, "We always are at the interface of quantitative data and qualitative understanding and FMEA is right at this interface."

G

Group think is usually associated with the pressures that a group can impose on its members. It attempts to homogenize thinking to a point that disagreements will be muffled, ore worse yet, just plain not allowed.

H

Hindsight bias occurs when an event has happened and we say we knew it was going to happen all along.

Heuristics "One central aspect of a heuristic is that it is blind to reasoning."[304]

Halo Effect This is the effect that occurs when we know certain things about someone and project that other unknown characteristics of this individual will be consistent with those already known. Since the word 'Halo' is associated with goodness, I use the term "Twisted Halo" to indicate our often mistaken thinking that if the person is known for some negative characteristic, we may assume other unknown characteristics are negative as well.

Heuristics are the quick and dirty rules that help us take short cuts to speed up our decision making. There are positive and negative aspects to the results they provide. The positive is usually the increased speed of our decisions while the negative is often seen as a bias.

I

Indirect test, page 172 of Baron. Direct tests of hypotheses look for confirmation, while indirect tests disconfirmation, falsification.

---

[304] Kalebfooled pg191

ICH Q9 The International Conference on Harmonisation of Technical Requirements for Registration of Pharmaceuticals for Human Use. Q9 is the Quality Risk Management guide.

Ikea effect occurs when we have put some effort into a product or process to make it more our own. The investment of time or other resources makes us reluctant to give up our venture for the same cost we paid in effort or money.

J K

L

Law of Averages see the law of large numbers.

Law of Large numbers. See Law of Small Numbers.

Lake Wobegon Effect (illusory superiority) is the bias that we have of overestimating our qualities. This reference comes from the radio show named the Prairie Home Companion where the fictitious town of Lake Wobegon is characterized in part by "where the children are all above average."

Law of Small numbers. This law is a misconceived version of the Law of Large numbers or Law of Averages which states that a sufficiently large series of numbers can be used to represent the population they came from or the process by which they were derived. While the same is not true for small numbers, we act as if it did.

M

Myside Bias is the tendency of people to favor information that confirms their beliefs

Types of *Memory*

Psychologists often make distinctions among different types of memory. There are three main distinctions:

1. Implicit vs. explicit memory
2. Declarative vs. procedural memory
3. Semantic vs. episodic memory

Implicit vs. Explicit Memory

Sometimes information that unconsciously enters the memory affects thoughts and behavior, even though the event and the memory of the event remain unknown. Such unconscious retention of information is called implicit memory.

Example: *Tina once visited Hotel California with her parents when she was ten years old. She may not remember ever having been there, but when she makes a trip there later, she knows exactly how to get to the swimming pool.*

Explicit memory is conscious, intentional remembering of information. Remembering a social security number involves explicit memory.

Declarative vs. Procedural Memory

Declarative memory is recall of factual information such as dates, words, faces, events, and concepts. Remembering the capital of France, the rules for playing football, and what happened in the last game of the World Series involves declarative memory. Declarative memory is usually considered to be explicit because it involves conscious, intentional remembering.

Procedural memory is recall of how to do things such as swimming or driving a car. Procedural memory is usually considered implicit because people don't have to consciously remember how to perform actions or skills.

Semantic vs. Episodic Memory

Declarative memory is of two types: semantic and episodic. Semantic memory is recall of general facts, while episodic memory is recall of personal facts. Remembering the capital of France and the rules for playing football uses semantic memory. Remembering what happened in the last game of the World Series

Memory, it's not what it used to be.

N

Natural frequencies (Counts, Gigerenzer) 5 people out of 1000 vs 0.5%

O

Occam's razor is a principle that advises one not to make an already sufficient explanation more complex. All else being equal, chose the simpler of competing theories that each adequately explain a problem

P

Priming acts by bringing closer to mind ideas associated with the suggestion or anchor.

Shermer pg 60 *patternicity* . . . "the tendency to find meaningful patterns in both meaningful and meaningless noise."

Taleb Black pg 303 "*Platonicity*: the focus on those pure, well-defined, and easily discernible object like triangles, or more social notions like friendship or love, at the cost of ignoring those objects of seemingly messier and less tractable structures."

Q

R

Representative heuristics are one of the short cuts we use to make estimates or probabilities. They function by estimating how close our problem is to another problem. For example, when comparing a series of numbers to another series, the question may arise as to which one appears more random. For example, Joe is a shy person. Is it more likely that he is a librarian or a politician? While librarian appears to be more consistent with the little we know about him, there are many more politicians than librarians in the area where he lives, but that important fact is often overlooked in our speedy decision.

S

The *Spotlight Effect* is the belief that you are the focus of everyone else's attention

K2011 pg 331 "*Salience* is enhanced by the mere mention of an event, by its vividness, and by the format in which probability is described . . ."

Spinoza's conjecture. Spinoza was a 17th-century philosopher who claimed that disbelief is more difficult than belief because prior to disbelieving you must first take the step of believing. So believing and disbelieving both require the step of believing; disbelieving adds a step of changing from belief to disbelief.

"*Suggestion* is the word we use when someone causes us to see, hear, or feel something by merely bringing it to mind." For System 1, where suggestion is equivalent to anchoring, "Suggestion[305] is a *priming* effect, which selectively evokes compatible evidence."

Silent evidence is the background information, such as a base rate, that is unfortunately, commonly disregarded when performing probability estimates.

In System 1, the anchor serves to automatically *prime* related ideas and ". . . evoke compatible evidence. "K2011 pg 122. These anchors need not be numerical. For example, the

---

[305] K2011 pg 122 "*Suggestion* is the word we use when someone causes us to see, hear, or feel something by merely bringing it to mind." "*System 1* tries its best to construct a world in which the anchor is the true number. This is one of the manifestations of associative coherence that I [Kahneman] described in the first part of the book."

anchor word "expensive" is more likely to bring to mind (*priming*) a new Mercedes Benz than an old Volkswagon. *Priming* acts by bringing closer to mind ideas associated with the suggestion or anchor.

From Kahneman's Nobel presentation, pg 450 "The operations of *System 1 (intuitive)* are fast, automatic, effortless, associative and difficult to control or modify. The operations of *System 2 (rational)* are slower, serial, effortful, and deliberately controlled . . ."

System 1 Is not prone to doubt. It suppresses ambiguity and spontaneously constructs stories that are as coherent as possible. K2011 pg 114. We are unaware of it. Some of its descriptors are: Experiential, Unconscious, Nondeclarative.

System 1 is gullible and biased to believe (K2011 pg 81) and we are unaware of it.

System 1/2 "the emotional tail wags the rational dog" K2011 pg 140

System 1 pg 105 K2011 "Links a sense of cognitive ease to illusions of truth, pleasant feelings, and reduced vigilance." "Neglects ambiguity and suppresses doubt" "Biased to believe and confirm" "Ignores absent evidence WYSIATI" "Sometimes it substitutes an easier question for a difficult one (heuristics)"

System 1 pg 114 K2011 System 2 is capable of doubt, because it can maintain incompatible possibilities a the same time. Unlike System 1, it can know what it doesn't know.

System 1 . . . K2011 pg 79 Jumping to conclusions is efficient if the conclusions are likely to be correct and the costs of an occasional mistake acceptable, and if it saves much time and effort. Jumping to conclusions is risky when the situation is unfamiliar, the stakes are high, and there is no time to collect more information. These are the circumstances in which intuitive errors are probable, which may be prevented by a deliberate intervention of System 1.

System 2 is in charge of being skeptical, doubting, and unbelieving. System 1 is gullible and biased to believe, biased to confirm.

306System 1 is effortless, automatic, associative, rapid, parallel process, opaque (i.e., we are not aware of using it), emotional, concrete, specific, social, and personalized.

1System 2 is effortful, controlled, deductive, slow, serial, self-aware, neutral, abstract, sets, asocial, and depersonalized.

S1 (System 1) The subconscious mind. Kahneman uses this classification extensively in his book, Thinking, Fast and Slow. I like to think of S1 as a primitive system that has maintained its necessity along with the recently developed S2.

S2 (System 2) The conscious mind. This more recent addition to our mind's systems for understanding the world seems like the only system, because S1 is noticed when it has sensed that things have significantly changed which turns out to be not that often.

For *System 2*, the anchor starts the deliberate adjustment process of moving away from the anchor towards an accepted value. A high anchor will lead one group to decrease its estimate, just as a group given a low anchor will adjust upwards. The important conclusion is that

---

306   Taleb Fooled pg 196

the adjustments are insufficient to arrive at an accurate judgment. K2011 pg 121 ". . . a well-intentioned child who turns down exceptionally loud music to meet a parent's demand that it be played at a 'reasonable' volume may fail to adjust sufficiently from a high anchor, and may feel that genuine attempts at compromise are being overlooked."

The following is from Type 1 error. http://www.intuitor.com/ statistics/T1T2Errors.html gives a very nice review of type 1 and type 2 errors in the justice system.

Briefly put:

"*Type I errors:* Unfortunately, neither the legal system or statistical testing are perfect. A jury sometimes makes an error and an innocent person goes to jail. Statisticians, being highly imaginative, call this a type I error. Civilians call it a travesty.

In the justice system, failure to reject the presumption of innocence gives the defendant a not guilty verdict. This means only that the standard for rejecting innocence was not met. It does not mean the person really is innocent. It would take an endless amount of evidence to actually prove the null hypothesis of innocence.

Type II errors: Sometimes, guilty people are set free. Statisticians have given this error the highly imaginative name, type II error.

Americans find *type II errors* disturbing but not as horrifying as type I errors. A type I error means that not only has an innocent person been sent to jail but the truly guilty person has gone free. In a sense, a type I error in a trial is twice as bad as a type II error. Needless to say, the American justice system puts a lot of emphasis on avoiding type I errors. This emphasis on avoiding type I errors, however, is not true in all cases where statistical hypothesis testing is done.

In statistical hypothesis testing used for quality control in manufacturing, the type II error is considered worse than a *type I*. Here the null hypothesis indicates that the product satisfies the customer's specifications. If the null hypothesis is rejected for a batch of product, it cannot be sold to the customer. Rejecting a good batch by mistake—a type I error—is a very expensive error but not as expensive as failing to reject a bad batch of product—a type II error—and shipping it to a customer. This can result in losing the customer and tarnishing the company's reputation.

Synapse : The junction between nerve or other cells that communicate chemically or electrically.

T

System 1 Intuit pg 57 (Dictionary of Philosophy of Mind) "*Tacit knowledge*, is not ordinarily accessible to consciousness"-it is intuitive. *Tacit* knowledge is procedural. Unlike explicit knowledge—knows that—tacit knowledge "knows how". "We know more than we can tell." Michael Polanyi

U

V

Plous Pg125 "*Vividness* usually refers to how concrete or imaginable something is, although occasionally it can have other meanings. Sometimes vividness refers to how emotionally interesting or exciting something is, or how close something is in space or time"

Valence Plouspg134 ". . . the degree to which an outcome is viewed as positive or negative." We tend to rate positive events as more probable.

W

WYSIATI What You See Is All There Is, an acronym from Kahnemann 2011 to express the limitations of how System 1 constructs and presents information to System 2. No analysis here, just observations. Also, what is not happening is beyond the capabilities of System 1.

X Y

References

"Some men's words I remember so well that I must often use them to express my thought. Yes, because I perceive that we have heard the same truth, but they have heard it better." Ralph Waldo Emerson.

1. Nobel Speech . . . Get URL for 2002 Economic's Nobel
    TO CITE THIS PAGE:
    MLA style: "Daniel Kahneman—Prize Lecture". Nobelprize.org. 6 Jul 2011 *http://nobelprize.org/ nobel_prizes/economics/laureates/2002/kahneman- lecture.html*
2. *http://www.ralentz.com/old/space/feynman-report.html,* Feynman's Appendix to the Rogers Commission Report on the Space Shuttle Challenger Accident
3. Blink, Malcom Gladwell 2005
4. The Folly of Fools 2011 Rober Trivers 2011
5. The Black Swan Nassim Nicholas Taleb, 2007
6. The Psychology of Judgment and Decision Making, Scott Plous, 1993
7. Visual Explanations, Edward R. Tufte, 1997,
8. Rationality for Mortals, Gigerenzer, 2008

9. On Being Certain, Burton, 2008
10. Thinking Fast and Slow, Kahneman, 2011
11. What Makes Your Brain Happy and Why You Should do the Opposite, DiSalvo, 2011
12. Fooled by Randomness, Taleb, 2004
13. Why We Make Mistakes, Hallinan, 2009,
14. Thinking and Deciding, Baron, 2008
15. Inevitable Illusions, How Mistakes of Reason Rule our minds. Piattelli-Palmarini, 1994
16. Gut Feelings, Gigerenzer, 2007
17. On Second Thought, Wray Herbert,
18. The Believing Brain, Shermer, 2011
19. The (Honest) Truth About Dishonesty, Ariely, 2012
20. Predictably Irrational, Ariely, 2008
21. How We Decide, Lehrer, 2009
22. Incognito, Eagleman, 2011
23. Judgment Under Uncertainty, Edited by Kahneman et. al. 1982
24. Intuition, Myers, 2002
25. Risk Intelligence, Evans, 2012
26. Proofiness, Seife, 2010
27. Once Upon a Number, Paulos, 1998
28. Don't Believe Everything You Think, Kida, 2006
29. Calculated Risks, Gigerenzer, 2002
30. Being Wrong, Schulz, 2010
31. Natrella

www.ingramcontent.com/pod-product-compliance
Lightning Source LLC
Chambersburg PA
CBHW030425290526
45786CB00001B/141